ORDINARINESS and LIGHT

ORDINARINESS
and LIGHT

Urban theories 1952-1960 and their
application in a building project 1963-1970

ALISON AND PETER SMITHSON

THE M.I.T. PRESS
Cambridge, Massachusetts

ISBN 0 262 19082 6

Library of Congress catalog card number: 77–125354

Printed in Great Britain

*A*t five o'clock, while the police of the Eighth Arrondissement were keeping an eye on the Mouse's movements, Lognon was ringing on the doorbell of a flat in the Avenue du Parc-Montsouris. It was on the sunny side of the avenue, and he was dazzled, as soon as he entered, by the brightness of the flat, with its white walls, its gaily coloured curtains, and its furniture which was so clean that it looked as if it had come straight from the shop.

A little boy of five was playing on the balcony. As for Lucile Boisvin, who was dressed in bright colours too, she no longer recalled the unruly child in the portrait, or the police reports, but suggested rather a model young mother, knitting with green wool.

As Lognon walked in without saying anything, with his stubborn look, she gave a start and asked:

'Did Edgar send you?'

Then, frightened by the bushy eyebrows which drew together, she said:

'Nothing's happened to him, has it?'

'I don't think so . . . I found this photograph in the neighbourhood . . . I wanted to give it back to you . . .'

She didn't understand.

'How did you know it was me?'

Then, rather embarrassed, he explained that he lived in the Rue Dareau, that he had already caught sight of her, and that he had thought that this photograph might have sentimental value for her.

As for her, nonplussed, she turned the piece of cardboard over and over between her fingers.

7

'It *was* Edgar, wasn't it, who told you . . .'

He felt uneasy, for he was not there on official business. He was in a hurry to get away . . .

'I just don't understand . . . This looks like the photo he insisted on keeping in his pocket . . . Tell me . . . You're sure nothing has happened to him . . .'

The child was listening to them. While Lucile Boisvin was dark, the boy had silver-blond hair and a milky-white complexion.

'Why hasn't he come?' she murmured as if to herself.

This visitor intrigued her. She had not asked him to sit down. It was warm, and Lognon reflected that he would have liked a flat as light as this one, without a single object lying around, without a single speck of dust, a flat which, in fact, made him think of a luxury clinic.

Georges Simenon *The Mouse* (*M. La Souris* 1938).
Translation by Robert Baldick p. 35–6: Penguin Books

Preface

The first part of this book was written in 1952–1953 at the time of the Korean War. Due to the world shortage of steel, there was a pause in general building activity. This pause seemed the right moment to try to set out as clearly as we could a basis for a new beginning.

Up to that time, the actual achievements in architecture and town re-building in England had been so feeble that for the ordinary person it was not possible to feel that any attempt to build the dreamed-of post-war world was being made. In the comprehensive redevelopment areas in London – Lansbury, Poplar for example – it was the same dreary old piecemeal tinkering of between the wars. Somehow a defeated world – and this was not the result of practical restrictions, it was a true bankruptcy of sustaining notions.

The 'New Towns' – by then several hundred thousand houses on the ground – were routine places, built to a common pattern. Not a single experimental housing area had been established, and no architect of our generation was given even six houses to do.

What could the authorities possibly have lost?

The extraordinary thing is that sixteen years later the situation has not really changed. Those same, now no-longer-young, men and women who studied with such dedication Le Corbusier's great housing experiment at Marseilles during its years of building between 1947–1953, still have not been allowed (with two bare exceptions) to attack the one problem that was central to their interest in their most formative period – that of housing.

For us personally the pause in building lasted from 1954 to 1962.

Re-reading this text now is both poignant and painful, for the sense of faith and of energy just waiting to be released can still be felt. In it were laid down the main themes we have been steadily working on ever since without conscious backward looks at what amounts to 'our

9

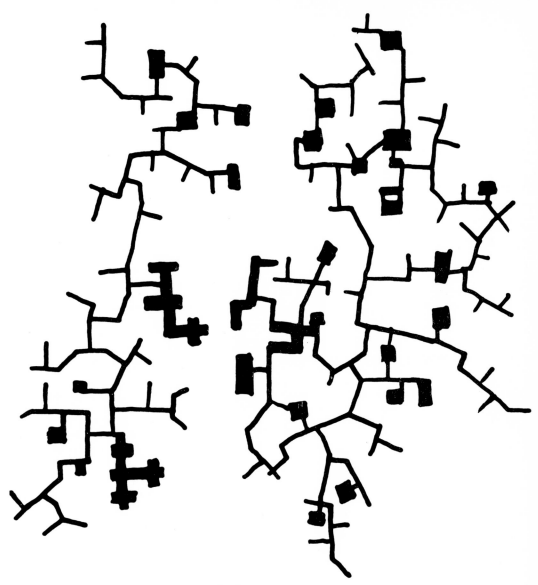

1. Reaching out to a random aesthetic

programme'; for the document – intended originally for publication as a
popular general statement of an idea (its format based on Le Corbusier's
classic work '*Urbanisme*') – was in fact never published as a whole, and
has lain unread over the intervening years.

It is a tumultuous rag-bag of a text, naive, embarrassingly rhetorical, but stuffed with good things.

Its survival, however, will not rest on the text but on the drawings; for in this work (the 'Golden Lane' study) was seen for the first time a random aesthetic reaching-out to town-patterns not based on rectangular geometries, but founded in another visual world.

This random aesthetic – or at any rate the graphics of it, if not an understanding of what it was reaching out towards – has since become part of the vocabulary of 'advanced' urban design all over the world, even down to the arrows on the drawings.

The main themes we still believe in passionately: the restoration of the feel of the land; the invention of an architecture structured by notions of association – of place; the re-direction of our cities and towns towards safe-movement, openness and light by inserting into the old structure urban events at the scale of our new patterns of communication.

It is published now in another pause in general building in England in the hope that it will yet catch the tide. For society is just beginning to experience the desolation of our environment. What we felt then, as professionals carrying the responsibility by default, with desperation and strong countering-energy, many ordinary people now also feel.

Acknowledgements

All the material in this book has been revised during the period 1966–1969 to eliminate repetition as far as possible, and to help sequential reading.

The authors and the publishers are grateful to the following photographers and sources for permission to reproduce illustrations: Aerofilms Ltd for plates 2, 34, 60, 91, 112, 114; The Ashmolean Museum, Oxford, for plate 58; The British Museum for plate 4; G. Douglas Bolton for plate 108; Emil Brunner, Braunswald, Switzerland, for plate 25; W. Boesiger of Zurich for plates 7, 76, 90 and 156, from the volumes of Le Corbusier's *Oeuvre Complète;* The City Librarian and Curator, Central Public Library, Edinburgh, for plate 11; P. H. Davis for plate 100; Fox Photos Ltd for plate 3; The Gernsheim Collection, University of Texas, for plate 105; Nigel Henderson for plates 21, 38, 69, and 80; Keystone for plates 50, 51 and 81; Felix H. Man for plate 63; The Ministry of Public Building and Works for plates 59 and 75; The National Gallery, London, for plate 62; Professor Vincent Scully for plate 79; The Radio Times Hulton Picture Library for plate 73; the U.S.I.S. for plate 137. A source-list for the illustrations, where traceable, appears on page 198.

We are also grateful to the Greater London Council for allowing the reproduction of drawings presented to their Housing Committee in 1967.

MacGibbon and Kee Ltd have allowed us to quote from Aneurin Bevan's *In Place of Fear,* which was originally published in 1952 by William Heinemann Ltd. Penguin Books Ltd permitted us to use the passage from *The Mouse* by Georges Simenon as an epigraph.

Contents

Urban re-identification

B   S.O.L.

1 The problem

*The task of our generation is plain – we
must re-identify man with his house
                    his community
                    his city*

'The Great Society has arrived and the task of our generation is to bring
it under control.'[1] We must make articulate the wants, the frustrations of
the individual by means of an architecture that has in it the seeds of a
different kind of city. We must answer the situation as it stands at the
moment. For young people there is the insoluble housing problem; for a
vast majority there is the time burden of one or more members of the
family commuting, and the attendant problem of how to include creatively
in society the wife left behind at home. For many of the lower middle
class there is little hope; they live in the ossified ring that surrounds every
town – the drab streets, the made-over Victorian and Edwardian terrace houses; few can qualify to be subsidised, the bigger the town the
fewer in proportion have council houses. The eyes of the general public
see the depressing sight of their money being used for drab tenements and
little boxes inundating the last fields near their homes.

We, more than any other people in the world today, have the adminis-
trative-economic set-up to make possible the large-scale re-building of
our cities; even in America, that wonder-land of anything possible, there
is no programme of new towns.

We have so far missed a great opportunity because no one any longer
has a clear idea.

'Before the rise of modern industrialism it could be said that the main
task of man was to build a home for himself in nature. Since then the

[1] Aneurin Bevan, *In Place of Fear*, p. 58.

18

outstanding task for the individual man is to build a home for himself in society . . . The individual today in the industrial nations is essentially an urban product. He is first a creature of his society and only secondarily of nature.'[2]

The drawing together that is London is a constant.
We have to build an urban environment for nearly all without covering any more agricultural land.

2. Lost farmland. Stevenage, Hertfordshire, 1952.

[2] Bevan, p. 56–7.

We must stop burying farmland, and fighting for an expensive and outmoded way of dwelling in a city. Fighting ourselves every day in our travel to work. Expensive in terms of our chances of survival.

Country is being separated from us: mere symbols are left. In every slum area small animals are kept; rabbits, pigeons, ferrets. We insist on keeping dogs in cities where they mess the streets. We see the country retreating up the Great North Road and scramble for a bit of land of our own – and away goes the country again like the fruit of Tantalus. You might argue that the back garden and front pocket handkerchief are necessary to look out on. But what fills the windows of your day rooms is the houses opposite and the backs behind. Do you really think this is a sustaining prospect?

How many of us honestly want a lawn as such, rather than a grass area to serve as a privacy-guard, an outdoor room, a secluded laundry green? How many gardens in your street are gardened for other reasons than that of keeping up 'appearances', and for how many is the possession of a garden at all not a personal solution but the only known answer for a civilised existence?

3. A home for oneself in nature. Farm on the Westmorland Fells, near Ullswater.

Is your home just what you'd build?

The argument that suburbs are what everyone wants is invalid.

We are not a mediaeval community that actually directs its individual houses to its taste. Folk-build is dead in England.

Manifesto of Antonio Sant' Elia July 14th 1914: 'Every generation to its own house.' Today's houses are like pianos, in the way in most lives. Housing for the man of today must be as different from his ancestors' houses as is the whole order of things.

4. The primeval mound of ancient Egyptian belief, with the scribe Ani as a swallow. Vignette from the Theban *Book of the Dead*, the Papyrus of Ani, XIXth Dynasty *c.* 1250 B.C. (British Museum)

In Egypt the creator was said to have emerged out of the waters of chaos and to have made a mound on which he could stand.

In the 1920's geometric pattern was to be the salvation of our cities. But applied pattern is a mere substitute for thinking: cities must remain organisms that each age can make its own while it inhabits them.

Ordered but not geometric.

Behind the geometric façades our washing, our china dogs and aspidistras look out of place. Life in action cannot be forced behind the netting of imposed pattern.

5. The *Highland Mary* taking on merrymakers for an afternoon jaunt on the Muskingum River, Ohio, 1894

'Modern industrial society is no longer a multiplication of a number of simple self-sufficient social groupings, each able to detach itself from the others without damage to itself. It is multicellular, not unicellular. Each part is connected as though by an infinite variety of nerves with all the others, so that separation is now a mutilation.'[3]

Our planners are patching. They make no attempt on the root problem.

Survey! preached Geddes.

Alas! the master never explained what happened next, or what you did with the survey once you had it.

We have not had a Haussmann or a Sixtus V, but we have had the industrialisation of the nineteenth century all over England. To do away with or not seize upon the scale of things it left us would be our equivalent

[3] Bevan, p. 68.

of doing away with the Place de la Concorde. In London we are ringed by railway stations and have the docks beyond the Tower. We must carry on this scale of thinking.

Whichever way a plan is drawn, ordered form should be apparent. Yet development plans for London reveal no form comparable to what exists. (So far only Lubetkin and Tecton at Busaco Street, near King's Cross, have seized on the new scale of things.)[4]

What use is the planner unless he makes order out of disarray and form out of the sea of building? Apart from the regiment of plans produced and the more laborious examination of the problem, we are comparably no further on from the Borough Surveyor, the Sanitary or Civil Engineer who did this work in the nineteenth century.

We can solve nothing by trying to lose a section of our inheritance, we cannot go back to the market town in our cities.

The architect or planner will be fortunate if he can add one genuine thing to a city. Let this thing be large or small it must be big in its

6. Potato shapes. 'Professor Sir Charles Reilly's plan. The houses are grouped around forty-four squares and potato-shaped greens, with club houses between. This is a plan for neighbourly living.' – from *The Architects' Journal*, August 3, 1944

[4] 1966. And Roehampton by the L.C.C. Architects' Department.

solution, its idea immediately apparent to the ordinary man so that each and everyone can re-orientate himself in relation to it.

A city is a living organism. You can feed it something new and it will renew and re-orientate itself accordingly; the process cannot be artificial or fake. However splendid the parks or museums, they only make more apparent by contrast the hopeless muddle round the home. No amount of community centres or culture clubs can make up for the fact that we have no ideal to build towards. We have lost the thought of the city itself as home.

Gone with the rocketing of Greater London to $8\frac{1}{2}$ millions is that last breath of the seasons. The unfortunates fill yesterday's single-family homes as though these were so many chests of drawers.

The city began to separate out into home streets and work streets when merchants ceased to live above their shops, as in John Gilpin's day, and retreated up the City Road to build in Islington. This was the beginning of a process which lead ultimately to the present total separation of home and work place. If our business men and civil servants had to make their homes in their disgraceful office buildings, the picture would be very different. Some would then take the care that the Louis took in choosing their architects.

The city need not be totally evacuated at weekends. City people could have the pleasures of the silence, feel the wind and sun across the city's surface as wind and sun on deserted flats or marshes.

Living and working are both changing and are not so incompatible: they should not be separated so laboriously in the future except in extreme circumstances. The attitude of segregation is a relic; not a little a relic of reaction to the overcrowded sewerless and smoky days[5] when few people in London can ever have felt entirely well.

The approach to a house is the occupants' link with society as a whole –

> a lengthy climb up a rickety stair or down into a basement
> up an avenue
> up an estate road
> along an air-conditioned artificially lit corridor.

These are man's links with society, the vistas down which he looks at his world; they frame his perspective view.

This is what really matters and not minimum room area, heights etc., etc., for any interior can be made a home, any place decorated or altered.

[5] *Circa* 1856.

24

But however clever the alteration or like a dream-house the interior, if one steps out into a corridor of an old block of singlewomen's flats in Abbey Road or goes down old house stairs in Notting Hill Gate, Paddington or Camden Town the dream world smashes, it is of no avail.

It is *not* sufficient to be an island of calm in a sea of chaos.

The path has been blazed by our international grandfathers.

Le Corbusier created ideal plans for the Paris and Algiers of his time, but it is London and other English cities that we need an ideal to build towards for our time.

7. Le Corbusier's plan for Algiers, project A, 1930

What of our New Towns that are actually building?

Corbusier or the 1920's might never have been. They are based on the plans of the time before last. The plans of the simple well-wishers, of the back to gentle nature era; ideas of English towns as off the mark as any English scene by Hollywood.

New Town development – query, find the new; query, find the town.

Was the idea of wishy-washy bands of housing trailing over the countryside – no doubt to a Morris dance – ever valid? Drive or walk into any example of the garden city idea and you will lose your sense of direction[6] in the wide streets that lead nowhere: wide tarmac rivers wave off in every direction, any of them may be the way out. Town Planners have written one rectangular clay-paper book after another on the relationship of house to church and house to vista-stop, and in practice completely missed the golden rule of satisfaction: a good road goes somewhere, a bad road does not. This is the holy hierarchy that has been so often tarmaced under into oblivion.

If a road is inadequate in spite of civil engineering it is because it once went nowhere and now somewhere has appeared at the end of it.

Not because more people have cars or that coaches were craftier or because all mediaeval men were 'gothic' or Anglo-Saxons had a life-long dislike of Roman directness.

8. Stone walls on moors. Yorkshire

In Lancashire and Yorkshire mills are set against the criss-cross of stone walls on moors. A block full of windows, the chimney, the water-tank, reservoirs and sluices reflecting in their juxtaposition the mills' contribution to the life of the area – bringing employment for farmers' daughters, extra money, power and services to areas that otherwise might still not have them.

Or a mill, a living tie of an area to its river. Originally the symbols were few and obvious, occurring often and speaking simply of clear-cut institutions; their local variation – water- or windmill, brick or stone church – able to inform.

Man must know his position.

One of the reasons why college and university life is enjoyable is that

[6] Harlow was readable at night because three different authorities were responsible for paths, town roads and main roads, and supplied three different types of lamp.

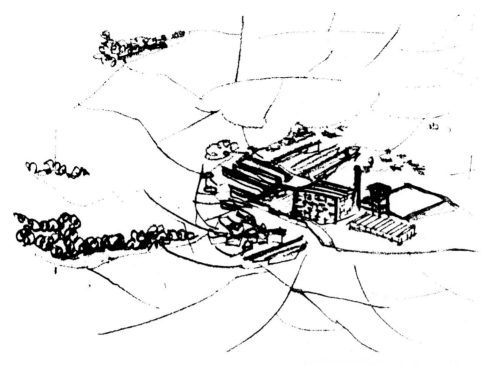

9. Mill in field pattern

10. The paper city of Holyoke, Connecticut.
The living tie of an area to its river

the student knows for this short period of his life his exact, therefore stable, position. He is at peace within his walls, able to react, to feel involved, committed. But in the outside world not only is stability withheld, life is fragmented.

Trappings and luxuries have far outstripped basic necessities. We lack essentials in accommodation but have television sets. Our portable comforts have blinded us to the fact that our houses have long been ridiculously mis-shaped for our lives and needs: that a public convenience has degenerated from a city to a hole in the ground. We are being buried alive by gadgets and ornaments in a civilisation whose cities lack homes, whose countryside is being buried. Farmland is squandered under southern New Towns when the very reason for the towns' being is, and remains, in London; towns built in the countryside to 'save' London, rather than because their presence there is vital and natural.

Surely positioning of towns should take into account the land, not just the nearest city's population? New Towns should be reserved for new countries where even the farms have yet to be made.

Is city sprawl natural growth? If farmers allowed this in their fields we would have nothing to eat but weeds. If doctors followed this principle there would be no patients left.

Why then do our city fathers deny the reason for their local government by allowing unprincipled growth? Our cities are allowed by irresponsibles to attack us, but the time will come when we will be forced to claim the country back.

But how does one do the work of hundreds of years? Make foodland out of our basements?

The functional city has been proposed and largely shouted down without many fully worked out exemplars. Diagrammatic development is barrenly vertical in our cities, like so many tombstones.

What we have seen built in such places as Glasgow and Liverpool shows us that had the brave new post-war world all appeared we would be more sadly lost.

The economic crisis has given us another chance.

Delacroix March 3rd 1824: 'Constantly exert yourself to return to great ideas.'

Demand a solution!
Demand a vacuum cleaner for your 'experts'!
The failure of nerve is everywhere.

28

Edinburgh which showed the world the vertical cramped mediaeval city taken to classical 'healthy' open sites, is now covering its surrounds with 'new' houses. Imagine the view as it was from the old vertical city, from the homes on the Royal Mile even after the George Street development had long been built, across to the Firth of Forth, itself amid country, to the hills of Fife beyond again.

11. Pre-1650 view of Edinburgh, by Rombout van den Hoyen

Yet today Edinburgh has abandoned the vertical city for a vast jumbled encampment in yesterday's cornfields below Craigmillar; even up the lower slopes of Arthur's Seat.

Is this mat of houses really an improvement on ribbon development? Now nobody can have unspoilt country, not even *The Scotsman* Calendar.

12. Dubrovnik, Yugoslavia; walled and moated for defence

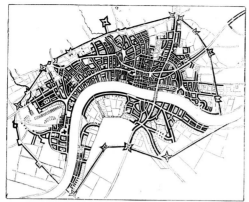 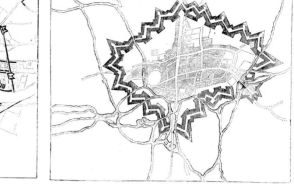

13. London 1643. Plan of the city and suburbs fortified

14. Plan of Oxford, with the Lines raised for its defence by Charles I

Our cities have slumped senseless and we have been irresponsible enough to let their sludge spread over the surrounding countryside.

It is vital we get some boundaries again. Once the towns were walled and moated for defence. Now the countryside must look to its defences against the creeping paralysis of the suburbs. It is as necessary as the Hollanders' fight against the sea.

We must erect our barricades and dykes.

2 The idea

We must contract our cities.

The choice between cottage and flat must be one between country and city. Otherwise the choice becomes one between the destruction or survival of the city.

It has been suggested that in our new towns families should be on the ground and single people high-up, but if the life lived high-up is worth living then it should be suitable for everyone who wants it. No taboo should be put on those with children, to live the lopsided existence of the suburbs; ostracised from town and country, forced into this antiquated way of life. We cannot afford to leave people scattered indiscriminately across the ground.

The spread town means delivery lines on the rack, stretched through corridor streets, putting fares up, causing waste of time.

Office workers can be fed straight into tubes and cars if need be, but why not live round the corner, or just across the park?

Future generations will find it hard to visualise the motive forces that sent masses traipsing out to the suburbs, wasting time of light and sun in transport vehicles.

Length of London bus routes – time taken to cross London – staggering!

What happens in the suburbs between 6 and 7 p.m.?

Visualise a roundabout at Hendon. We crawl up to it three deep, cars and vans shuffle for position. On the roundabout we get stuck. No policeman in sight, very law abiding out here, we wait. The odd driver gets out to look about and climbs back in. Twenty minutes pass. We shuffle round a bit, suddenly a car is popped out and we are off again, past several hundred yards of three-deep cars.

No doubt it will happen again this evening.

31

The old industrial areas linked men's houses with their work but not, as part of the objective, with the country. People today have gained fresher air and some quiet but they have to travel to work as well as to the country. We have lost membership of the town without gaining membership of the country in exchange. We have been neutralised into an 'in-between' position in these housing estates; unsatisfying and insipid largely because of their surface spread.

We have forced on ourselves, by our wasteful practices, an era when we must make strict economies. We are told to cut from our spaces every odd corner. We compromise functions by making rooms multi-purpose, spaces meaner, and we risk building the next decade's slums.

15. '*Househunter:* "No, I don't think this would do. I doubt if there's a room in the house large enough to swing a cat in!" *Agent to clerk:* "Parkins, just step across to Miss Singleton's – number 25 – and borrow a cat; any average kind will do." ' – *Punch* 1912

It would be better to go to the root of the matter and clump the functions of our towns. Let us cast aside the idea of letting areas of our cities lie fallow and deserted at nights, weekends and holidays.

Let us abandon the wasteful strip usage of our central areas. Let new homes change our cities, as turnips once changed the look and spirit of the landscape of England.

16. The minimal dwelling *c.* 1950. Tram hut at Blackfriars Bridge, London

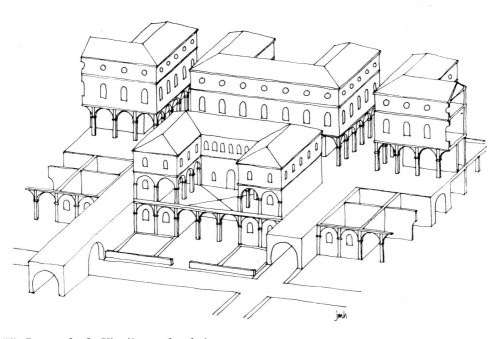

17. Leonardo da Vinci's two-level city

The attempt to contract towns is not new. Leonardo da Vinci designed a city whose pedestrian and service ways were separated – his two-level city. We must evolve the multi-level city.

Cars are the latest thing in style and our roads are generally good, but our houses are antiquated in spirit: many of the newest are the most arid. Family flats stuck up on a ledge with only five or six neighbours instead of the forty or fifty found in an old street.

We feel the need for the district, the pub at the corner. Because of shortsightedness why should we be cut off from our 'back yard', our sense of a bit of territory?

18. Islington, north London. Back-yard pattern

Without links with our fellows we are dead.

We must have our circle of friends, our district, without whizzing up and down and across to the next slab block.

Living high should not mean living like caged birds, but should provide what the old order had, with added views, privacy from over-looking, and safety of movement. Movement up and down as well as along and round the corner, so that our immediate neighbours are increased not decreased.

Why should we climb up into the towers when it should be possible to go round the corner for odds and ends, paper and 'phone calls and the postbox. Why for ever going up and down and along and up again when

34

we could all live on a quiet street-deck for pedestrians, young children, milkmen's trolleys, prams.

We can live at each level, not just be filed away there.

Not always crowding to the ground but living a full life round about as well as in our home.

19. Edinburgh. Pedestrian way behind the Royal Mile. A similar one exists above Leith Walk

20. London. Old three-storey walk-up

21. Bethnal Green, east London. Milk cart.

There will be insufficient room for our school fields, sports grounds and market gardens if we complicate traffic problems still more. People must not be tempted by the busy traffic to build on the ground and so spoil the terrific advantage that living on many levels can give. There must be no flaw for the speculator to find in our green-clothed ground. If we keep the basic idea unspoilt there will be no future problem of street widening and slicing of property, no queer-shaped sites and city problems. The ground really clears in the normal course of re-housing.

It all hinges on the housing solution; for already we have the department store and the multi-level garage for our high level street-deck ends.

The horizon clears.

Where can we hope to see this multi-level city?

Our cities are ringed with a decayed belt. In London tube travellers duck under all this as they make their entrances and exits, but those who travel on the surface find mile after mile of decayed and decaying dwellings between them and their work. Dingy remains of the first exodus from the cities.

England was one of the first countries to bring in housing laws. England always protects her citizens by law but too often it ends there, for men of vision in this field are rare: Jones, Vanbrugh, Hawksmoor; then no other men of genius in architecture since 1736. But the decayed belt must be cleared and rebuilt and our suburbs brought home.

CASE STUDY, LONDON. The south bank area was always something of a poor relation, even when the river was the main traffic artery.

From the City of that period you could see Harrow church on the hill. Away across fields in the distance were the ring of surrounding slopes; on them villages, hamlets, farms were dotted about. No drink could be had between the hamlet just off Tottenham Court Road, and the place where Dick Whittington looked back to the spiky patch that was the pre-fire City with over 120 churches. It was in those days the accepted idea that the City should be surrounded by a belt in which building was forbidden: no person could have the benefit of the City without being *of* the City (paying taxes, obeying the rules).

The fire really lost the cause of the first green belt. People camped in the fields, rented huts.

Wren's one achievement of a new-scaled urban space was a Dutch-type quay in Farringdon Road; but first fire rubbish was dumped by night

22. London Bridge *c.* 1616

on the quayside, then flooding from blocked and broken sluice gates up in Holborn, caused by 'suburban' domestic jetsam, made it necessary only 25 years afterwards to roof in this virtual sewer.

The Tower was still outside the City limits, and beyond it the Huguenots built in Bethnal Green, forming a new community *of* the City but with its own independent tensions. Just as Westminster always was a separate entity, destined through Parliament to create the London Season with its mass movements and life tempo. In spite of this the City was still thought of as all-dominant: the theatre area was termed the West End, although from their houses its patrons travelled east to it.

Wren and Evelyn were thwarted. Greater London is still recognisably the agglomerate of villages that grew together.

In the fields between the villages was built the new town of squares and streets. Organised on an additive basis which is peculiarly English.

The order of sameness of scale, colour, texture, life pattern and tempo, of post-fire and Georgian London was torn asunder by the Victorian effort. Houses as offices and shops no longer suited.

The Victorians had to invent new types of building and they were bored with Georgian London. The jump in space-scale must have required superhuman effort, and the invention of a new style at the same time is too much to have expected of them.

The spate of building immediately prior to 1927 was an even more violent disruptive change.

The prestige and cash went to the mammoth stores in Oxford Street; the original West-end became virtually a dirty crack between two cities.

London was cracked open. The first suburbs were abandoned for later and later ones as people jockeyed for position next to the fields.

There now awaits a belt of tired property which should be entirely stripped away, for the re-identified city to be created on its vast acreage.

These new homes and work places would form the renewed city walls, a vantage point from which to watch the suburbs of semi-detached houses shrivel and die.

We have to try to re-identify man with his environment – to arrive at an idea of city in which every building, every lamppost and street sign will seem part of a predestined harmony of which man is part.
All else is futile.

3 Human associations

What are we looking for?

Can we assume there is any ideal pattern of association?

In the vacuum – not knowing what to do – is it right to continue to build to an ossified living pattern?

Thoughts on providing housing are in the awful mess the Poor Laws once were.

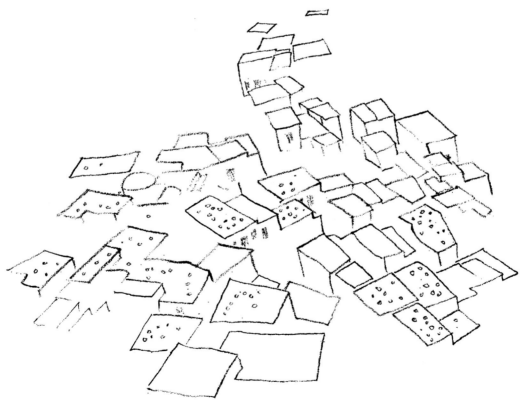

23. Skyros, Greece

24. Village in the Peloponnese

Things should not be different without reason.

Things of the same order should be as alike as leaves.

To construct an 'estate' where each house is different is not to identify but to destroy the possibility of them making greater sense together.

Houses are cells of districts, as districts are of towns, and without sameness houses will add up to nothing. A change of style or size in a house must be a symbol of a reality of social organisation, not a whim of 'town design'.

25. El Oued in the Sahara

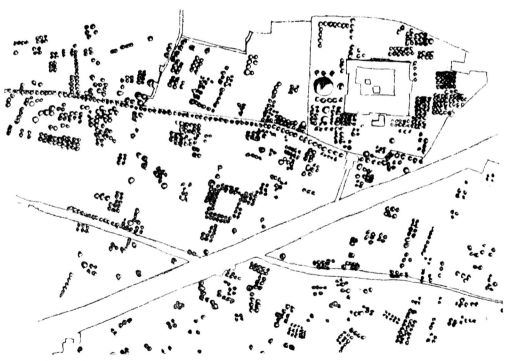

26. Isfahan, Iran

27. Matmata, Tunisia. Courtyards of subterranean dwellings

28. Honan, China. Subterranean settlement 30–45 feet down in the loess

'To the social psychologist society presents primarily a picture of a network of human relations. The strength and direction of those relationships not only determine the coherence and effectiveness of society – they also are the primary source of individual satisfaction. The function of social planning is primarily to strengthen and direct these relationships. . . . Town-planning theory, however, has tended to construct groups on a functional basis, round an infant school, a community centre or a group of shops. Such theories overlook the fact that the inhabitants may prefer a different school (for religious reasons, for instance), may prefer to shop in the centre of the town, or may prefer to make their social contacts at the swimming pool, chess club, or dance hall.'[7]

Thus social theory defines what we all know, that social groups are not created by location alone but by community of interest and physical and psychological interdependence. The family can still be tight-knit and possessive when its members are thousands of miles apart; the 'extended family' can be scattered through many districts and classes of a town; and the 'assessment group' of the intellectual or artist may be international and non-collingual, yet with more in common than with many neighbours.

The assumption that a community can be 'created' by geographic isolation is invalid.

Real social groups cut across geographical barriers, and the principal

[7] Rattray Taylor, *Architects' Year Book 4* 1952; p. 28, 29

aid to social cohesion is looseness of grouping and ease of communication rather than the isolation of arbitrary sections of the total community with impossibly difficult communications, which characterise both English neighbourhood planning and the Unité concept of Le Corbusier.

The creation of non-arbitrary groupings and effective communications are the primary functions of the planner. The basic group is obviously the family, traditionally the next grouping is the street (or square or green, any word that by definition implies enclosure or belonging; thus 'in our street' but 'on the road'), the next the district, and finally the city. It is the job of the architect and planner to make these groupings apparent as tangible realities.

In the suburbs and slums the vital relationship between the house and the street survives, children run about (the street is comparatively quiet), people stop and talk, dismantled vehicles are parked. In the back gardens are pigeons and so on, and the shops are round the corner: you know the milkman, *you* are outside *your* house in *your* street.

29. The shell that fits man's back.
Slovak peasant cottage

43

The house, the shell which fits man's back, looks inward to family and outward to society and its organisation should reflect this duality of orientation. The looseness of organisation and ease of communication essential to the largest community should be present in this, the smallest. The house is the first definable city element.

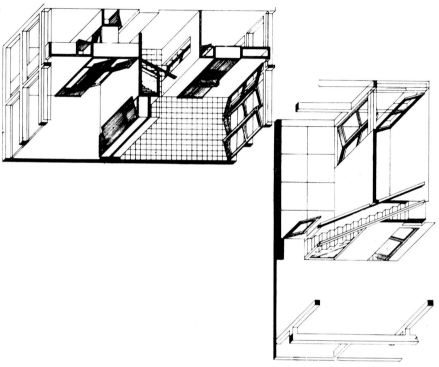

30. The shell that fits man's back. Golden Lane. Axonometric drawing of house cell

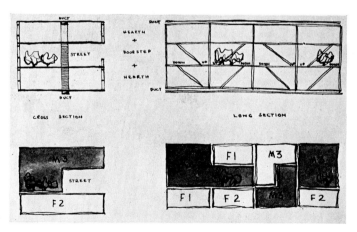

31. Golden Lane. House cell, diagrams

44

Houses can be arranged in such a way that a new thing is created – the 'street'.

The 'street' is our second definable city element.

The 'street' is an extension of the house; in it children learn for the first time of the world outside the family; it is a microcosmic world in which the street games change with the seasons and the hours are reflected in the cycle of street activity.

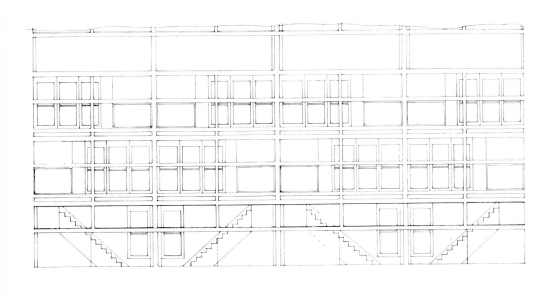

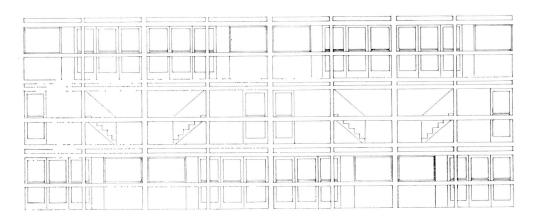

32. Elevations of part of the Golden Lane façade

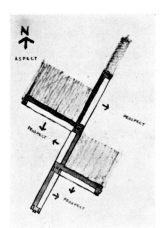

33. Golden Lane deck

But in suburb and slum, as street succeeds street, it is soon evident that although district names survive, as physical entities they no longer exist. But we all know that once upon a time those streets were arranged in such a way and with such additional things necessary to sustain life, that they formed the third definable city element, the district.

34. Air view of industrial houses in Burnley, taken in 1950

46

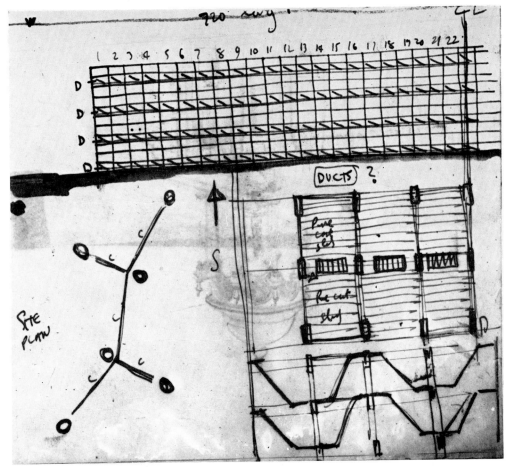

35. The original sketch of the Golden Lane idea. It is the idea of street, not the reality of street that is important

36. Golden Lane 'district'

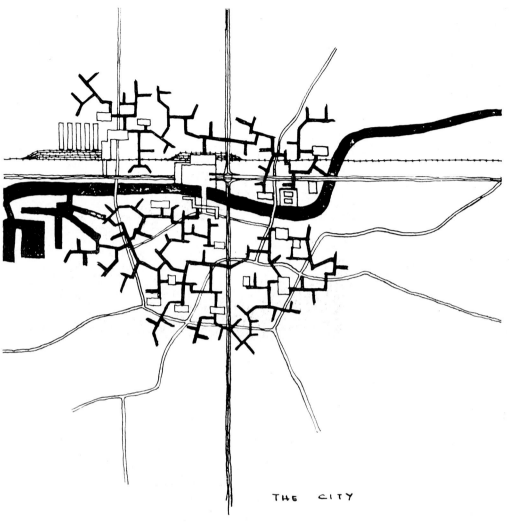

THE CITY

37. Golden Lane city

The difference between towns and cities is only one of size, for both are arrangements of districts.

The city is the ultimate community, 'the tangible expression of an economic region'.

It is extremely difficult to define the higher levels of association, but the street implies a physical contact community; the district an acquaintance community; and the city an intellectual contact community.

To maintain looseness of grouping and ease of communication, the density must increase as the population increases; and with high densities, if we are to retain the essential joys of sun, space and verdure, we must build high.

48

38. Nigel Henderson's drawing room, Bethnal Green, east London, 1952. Silk screen elements by Eduardo Paolozzi, used as wallpaper

39. Golden Lane street perspective

In the past the acceptance of the latter part of this thesis has led to a form of vertical living in which the family is deprived of its essential outdoor life, and contact with other families is difficult if not impossible on the narrow balconies and landings that are their sole means of com-

munion and communication. Furthermore, outside one's immediate neighbours (often limited to three in Point Blocks) the possibilities of forming the friendships which constitute the 'extended family' are made difficult by the complete absence of horizontal communication at the

51

same level, and the ineffectiveness of vertical communication.

The *idea* of 'street' has been forgotten.

It is the idea of street not the reality of street that is important – the creation of effective group-spaces fulfilling the vital function of identification and enclosure, making the socially vital life-of-the-streets possible.

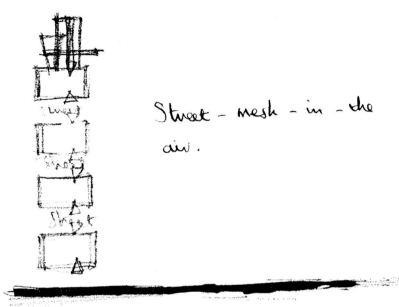

40. Street-mesh-in-the-air

At all densities such 'streets' are made possible, by the creation of a true street-deck in the air, each deck having a large number of people dependent on it for access, and some decks being thoroughfares – leading to places – so that they will each acquire special characteristics.

Be identified in fact.

Each part of each deck should have sufficient people accessed from it to become a social entity and be within reach of a much larger number at the same level.

Decks would be places, not corridors or balconies: thoroughfares where there are 'shops', post boxes, telephone kiosks.

Where a deck is purely residential the individual house and yard-garden will provide an equivalent life pattern to a true street or square; nothing is lost and elevation is gained.

The flat block disappears and vertical living becomes a reality.

The refuse chute takes the place of the village pump.

52

It is the custom of planners to adopt architecturally fashionable housing solutions as the basis for theoretical residential densities.

The classic case is the twelve houses to the acre, a density of rigorous social merit, giving the amount of land that an industrious artisan could work for profit in his spare time in 1912. Such a density (30–40 persons to the acre) is still the basis for the so-called 'open development' (magnificent views of next door's back garden).

Current planning theory assumes the pyramidal density structure of the Victorian town to be based on a social reality worth perpetuating. 1944 Housing Manual: 'In general, the nearer the centre the higher the density:

Open development	*30–40 persons per acre*	
Outer ring of a town	*50–60* ,, ,, ,,	
Inner ring of a town	*75* ,, ,, ,,	
Central areas	*100* ,, ,, ,,	
Central areas/large towns	*120* ,, ,, ,,	

As we have all seen, the results of such densities have been disastrous.

On the smallest scale, miners housed at 30 to the acre have two gardens (front and back) which only one in ten is prepared even to pretend to cultivate (after a shift labouring how many want to dig potatoes with £30 in their back trousers pocket?). In the larger towns the increase in travelling distance materially affects the poorer worker.

High buildings are only tolerated 'to enable as large a number of two and three storey houses as possible to be built in such areas'. (Housing Manual again.)

In the County of London Plan, 1943, three degrees of density were adopted, 100, 136 and 200 persons to the acre, the smallest area in the centre having 200 to the acre, then a larger area of 136, and finally the outer areas at 100. These areas were adjusted to give an overall density of 136 to the acre, producing the maximum estimated absorbable overspill of 600,000 persons. This overspill was to be absorbed in satellite towns whose existence, as the name implies, depended on the city itself and whose realisation is at variance with the principle of maximum convenience and minimum locomotion which were the objects of the plan.

In 1952 we produced a competition project for rehousing an area of Central London in accordance with the principles of Urban Re-Identification.

This Golden Lane project was rejected.

The Golden Lane site is part of an area known as Bunhill Fields, which was scheduled for Comprehensive Development by London County Council. It had been almost completely razed by bombing and had been used as a tip for blitz rubble. The ground level prospect at the time of the competition was a dismal one of blighted Peabody Trust dwellings and multi-storey buildings. There are no fields on Bunhill now, but there is a magnificent high level view to the south of St Pauls and the Pool of London.

The gross area of the competition site, including portions of surrounding street, was 4·7 acres. The population density approved for the site was 200 persons per acre. The population was to be calculated on the basis of 1·1 persons per habitable room and as many dwellings as possible (of various given types) had to be provided.

Within this framework and with strict regard to economy we tried to prove that living at high densities does not necessarily mean low standards; that an infinitely richer and more satisfactory way of living in cities is possible here and now; and that this did not need the demolition of whole areas but could be built on individual sites as they became available.

To do this we proposed three levels of 'streets-in-the-air', each level we called a 'deck'. Off each 'deck' would live 90 families, with their group activity concentrated in two square crossings at the street intersections. These crossings are triple height, contrasting with the single height decks, inviting one to linger and pass the time of day. There are stairs and lifts at these crossings and deck ends (which are similarly triple height).

All dwellings have their front doors on deck level and their main accommodation above or below deck.

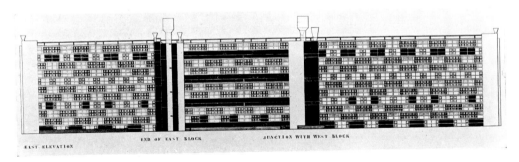

EAST ELEVATION   END OF EAST BLOCK   JUNCTION WITH WEST BLOCK

41. Golden Lane elevation

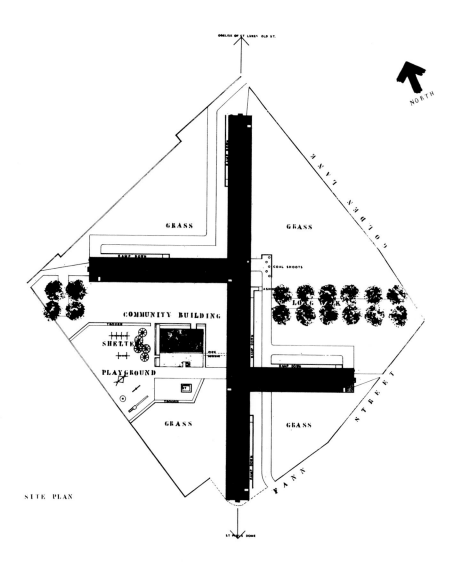

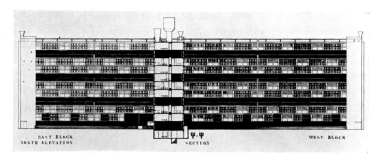

42. Golden Lane elevation, section and site layout

The BASIC UNIT (parents' apartment) is standard in all dwellings in the scheme, and varying sizes of families can be accommodated in ADDITIONAL BEDROOMS (children's) at deck level. With these additional bedrooms are the yard-gardens – 16′ 0″ × 8′ 0″ when there are two additional bedrooms (type M4). The majority, but not all, dwellings have yard-gardens.

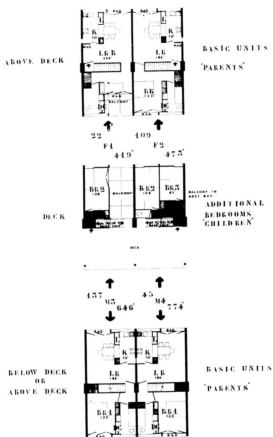

43. Golden Lane house plans. Note: all dwellings consist of a standard basic unit, with additional bedrooms at deck level as required

These yard-gardens, which can be seen from the deck, bring the out-of-doors life of a normal house – gardening, bicycle cleaning, joinery, pigeons, children's play, etc., on to the deck, identifying the families with their 'house' on their deck. The arrangements at deck level are 'detached', 'semi-detached' or 'terraced' (each deck differs). The piece of the dwelling at deck level is small and unintimidating to the playing child, and the passing stranger's view is enriched by glimpses, through the open yard-gardens, of the city and river.

44. Golden Lane yard garden, 16 by 8 feet

These pedestrian decks are no mere access balconies. Two women with prams can stop and talk without blocking the flow, and they are safe for small children, as the only wheeled vehicles allowed are the tradesmen's hand- and electrically-propelled trolleys.

The decks in the competition project have the following pattern:

GROUND	4 and 1 person dwellings
FIRST DECK	4 and 2 ,, ,,
SECOND DECK	3 ,, ,,
THIRD DECK	3 and 2 ,, ,,

This arrangement is such that any vertical section of the complex contains dwellings in the same proportion as in the whole, but as the same standard units occur throughout it can be varied to suit local needs.

The use of the houses as house-shops and house-workshops will not interfere with the normal working of the plan, as there is always the possibility of two 'front doors'. The yard-garden can be used as an alternative means of access, or for a market-stall.[8]

[8] 1966. Alternative use only works if the servicing and deliveries are at a primitive level.

As far as the appearance of the complex is concerned it would be enhanced rather than destroyed by such changes. The patterns of the façade are the result of logical disposition of the parts in accordance with a consistent social attitude – the order is based on living patterns not architectural ones.

To reflect the continuity of the street deck the blocks flow into one another with an uninterrupted articulation, which the expansion joints punctuate according to their own laws. The total penetration of the yard-gardens dissolves the dead-wall effect of the conventional slab block, and produces ever-changing vignettes of life and sky; the individual dwelling clearly being the measure and reason for the whole.

People are its predestined ornament.

45. Golden Lane, vignette patterns of life and sky

The setting-up of such a deck system would be like establishing the lines of the main sewers. A 'deck-law' would make provision for pedestrian streets at specified levels.

No building would have its major pedestrian entry point on the ground.

Going to the ground would be a small event, like going to the cinema, to school, to the office, or to play tennis, a special journey for a special purpose.

Access to roads would be through multi-level garages and parking ramps.

The public entrances of some shops and offices could be directly off pedestrian decks.

Ways-in-the-air could be a framework, like drains, to which everyone connects up. They would be a fixed fact no more cramping than other public services, but sufficiently revolutionary to make urban re-organisation a fact, to make re-identification a fact, and the organisation of the fact possible. It would be almost like passing a law against the construction of out-of-date buildings, for the 'aesthetic' of this school and that would be subdued, and their stock answers no longer applicable.

46. Sea dayaks' long house. Some houses are a quarter of a mile long and hold ninety families

Whether or not the optimum density of such residential development is 200 to the acre is difficult to decide.[9] With a completely developed district, London planning legislation daylight standards can be maintained at twice the height of the Golden Lane project, and certainly with fully

[9] 1966. On density: we now think that 150 persons to the acre is sufficient, by the 'feel' and 'smell' of such densities. Probably in most cases 100 to the acre would 'feel normal' at present levels of car ownership and servicing.

developed shopping thoroughfares, multi-level garages and other district facilities, and the clearing of ground completely, heights of up to 150 feet will be necessary. But commonsense suggests a top limit of about 200 feet in residential areas, for winds at these heights are already formidable.[10]

The leaves on the trees should still be recognisable from our topmost dwellings.

In offices, shops, hotels, etc., where the deck is no longer necessary as a social space, American experience suggests that there is *no* height limit structurally or psychologically.

The deck system would slot into the vertical circulation of such complexes.

This could be the pattern of our large cities.

47. Golden Lane study, street deck complex. The street mesh slots into the vertical circulation of such complexes

But in villages and small towns the law of density and size will operate against high building. For what can be the possible merit of a multi-level development when the community has a small population? Height would hinder ease of circulation, and to lose contact with the gardens and fields

[10] 1966. These heights for open-deck systems are probably excessive. It is likely that only below 100 feet are they practicable for normal locations.

without gaining the advantage of intense human association (which is city) is fatuous. Perhaps one would in such cases only live high in special circumstances of land value and location. But certainly the quite arbitrary and mutually compromising close mixture of flats and houses in our New Towns should be anathema.

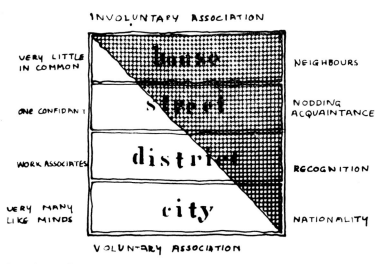

48. Hierarchy of association

In villages and towns the important problem is to find solutions to 'street' and 'district' which fit more closely our real living patterns. The village green, the square, and the terraced street are historic forms of association, answers to problems quite different from our own, and it is at just this level – defining the patterns of association in a mechanised and non-demonstrative society – that we have failed most significantly. But this document is concerned with the *urbs* proper – where the problem of re-identification is most urgent, and to this we must return.

4 Communications and dispositions

It is not surprising that while the well documented 'space-time' concept of the Modern Movement in architecture is an academic commonplace, the real space problems of the twentieth century are unrecognised and unsolved. For the conceptual step involved is a great one.

The nineteenth century made immense scale changes with the revolution of the railways and canals and all they involve.

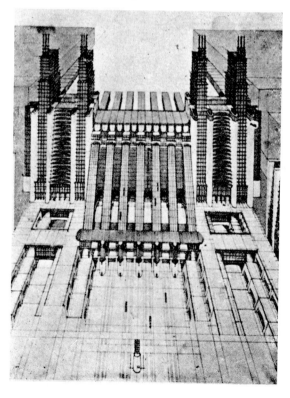

49. Antonio Sant' Elia. Central Station of the Città Nuova, 1913–14

62

We are faced with scale changes consonant with the internal combustion engine, with road and air transport.

The internal combustion engine has created the world city and the world city scale. We are in truth being asked to make human a new vastness! A problem so difficult that the sooner we start on it the better.

We must live our lives on different levels. For cities of high density a new form of transport is essential. Always to go to the ground for local transport – trolleys, trams, short distance buses – would be tedious, and the actions of doing so would be the negation of the idea of life at each and every level.

How then are our homes to be linked to the greater organism?

It is out of the question to carry our roads up to higher levels. With road loads increasing daily, the heavy transport must be kept on the ground and our pedestrian levels linked to the delivery points and terminals. Lifts up to our pedestrian decks are today's answer, but vertical travel is still Victorian in mechanics and conception. Purely from the practical standpoint new vertical transport must be made more reliable

50. A helicopter landing with Epiphany gifts in front of Milan Cathedral, 1950

than lifts, and give a more continuous service. We can only pose the question, which is for our transport engineers to answer. It is not the first time that new forms of transport have made new forms of city life practicable: with the invention of the lift – the skyscraper.

51. Little Henry 1949. The first American jet helicopter on a test flight

Before 1900 office workers walked to work, pouring over London Bridge, in from the home streets, down the City Road. All the people walked. There were no school buses but the children came home for lunch all the same. Then, even with the tenements and flats, London filled up and the distance away of the new suburbs made walking ridiculous. The early steam locomotive underground, horse trams, Tilling's buses, made commuting possible.

For our present-day regional cities the system of travel must be re-thought.

In old towns and villages the pattern of inter-relationships from the house to the region is always made clear in the road system. One is informed of being at the centre or at the periphery, or of whether the road one is standing on goes somewhere or nowhere and just how important that somewhere or nowhere is.

This sure sense of location and orientation is at the root of the well-being one has in a mediaeval town.

Railways and canals cutting uncompromisingly through countryside and town follow their own laws and extend our sense of location beyond the region to whole continents. Today the international airlines tracking high over our heads on invisible roads locate us in a network of world relationships.

But on the ground there is chaos. The whole traditional structure has been lost in a sea of compromise, and a city street may be the Great North Road or the back access to a corner shop.

That the road system is inefficient at this level and therefore chaotic is a commonplace, but inefficiency and chaos operate at a far deeper level of man's need than turn-around times and optimum road speeds.

The creation of a significant road hierarchy is fundamental to identity.

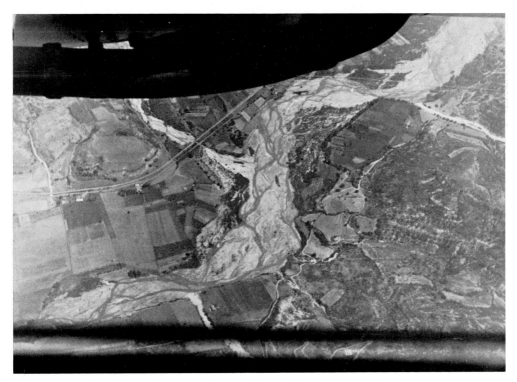

52. Beware aircraft crossing

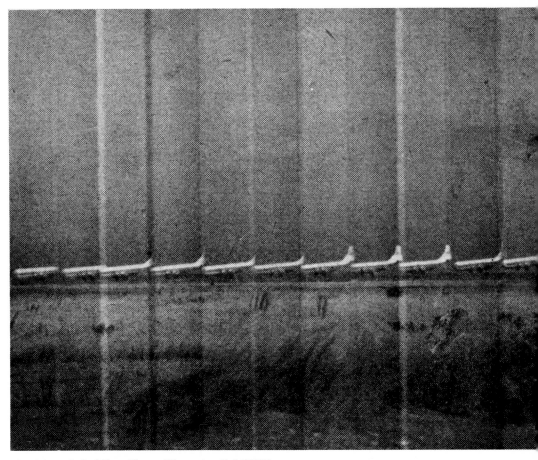

53. Aircraft landing (from *Time*, April 6 1953)

It is important to be open-minded about the construction of a new transport system to serve our pedestrian decks. We may find that a revolutionised railway system, or the use of helicopters for local high speed passenger services, will make our proposed 120 foot wide 'ring roads' ridiculous.

It is the urbanist's duty to remind engineers of the symbolic function of roads, and to see that techniques do not ignore ends.

Beware of cattle crossing,
      aircraft crossing,
        pedestrians crossing.
Danger from deer,
      from helicopters?

We must live our lives on different levels, leaving on the ground only

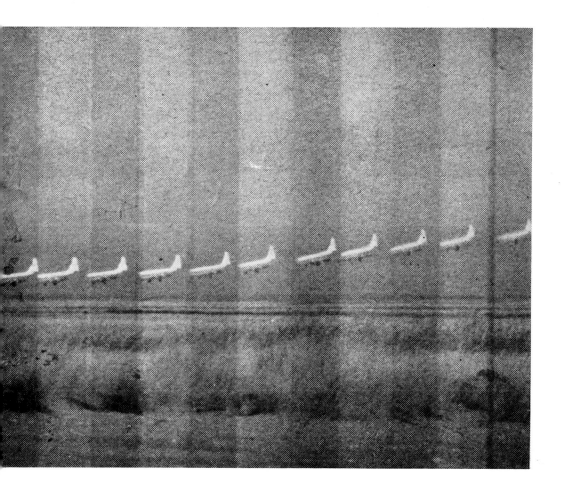

things which are tied – heavy and long-distance transport lines, road, rail, water – for the rest, tried space solutions are available.

In large cities such things as light industries, workshops, clinics, shopping centres and small hotels, could easily be located on raised levels; integrated with the deck-dwelling pattern.[11]

But things like markets and big stores present special problems. For in their essence they are large-area horizontal activities, and consideration of such activities and of similar ones may well provide the key to the patterns of ground elements.

The large office buildings, hospitals,[12] hotels and shops will be linked

[11] 1966. Providing always that their servicing does not compromise the dwellings.
[12] 1966. Le Corbusier, just before his death, made his design for the hospital of Venice where the streets and waterways of the city unobtrusively became the routes of the hospital and its chapel.

54 Graveyard, Houmt Souk, Djerba

with the pedestrian deck system in an unemphatic manner. The existing solutions of Rockefeller Center, Waldorf and Bon Marché could be given new flexibility and point by being connected to statutory deck levels.

Car parking could (at a price) be at any level the driver wishes to visit, parking ramps forming the core of the department stores or similar, following the idea of the drive-in store in America.

'One of the most fascinating sidelights on the story of mankind is the gulf which persisted between urban illumination and the twilight behind . . . The country was exploited by the town and could not share in what the town could give it . . . Where the countryside is neglected it always takes its revenge. Unless country and town march together in reciprocal activity, civilisation will limp on one foot.'[13]

We must all be able to feel the land, not just those in the last new house in the suburbs. Land flowing under our noses; parks, greens, and market gardens.

We need grand parks and gardens where the city is most intensely used, and green spaces near all houses. For if hours of labour are to go on

[13] Bevan, p. 60.

being reduced, greater facilities for recreation must be provided. The extension of the free time saved from travel to homes must not be nullified by travel to play. Outdoor recreation should be within walking distance of each home. And to expect market gardens right at the back door of our greengrocers is perhaps not ridiculous. Progress in horticulture in recent years has been rapid. In equipment in the last ten years, and in sprays in the last five years, this advance has been timely enough for market gardening to play its part vigorously in the reclaiming of our cities. Farming could advance in this form before the city fully retreats.

We have only to give the signal.

The country is waiting under London; willow-herb watching its time in the blitzed basements: squirrels, owls, wood pigeons, even bats still inhabit central London squares and parks.

At the new city scale making a garden should be like making a range of hills.

Hills are a great formal idea, ever various, expressive of mood, expectant of weather. Today we might make contour relief by means of the same earth shifting equipment that opencasts coal.[14] Only this scale of modelling is bold enough to tell from above at the new city scale of things. 'Capability' Brown raised eyes from the parterre to rove among fine silhouetted trees, over undulating fields and inviting screens of woodland. We will be lowering our eyes to look down from our street-decks and homes; another dimension entering our lives.

The land must be reclaimed, even if resistance squads have to plant ivy in people's gutters.

The bulldozer that has been employed to ruin quickly can be employed to make quickly. It can attack the pre-war jerry-built houses; and ultimately the Housing Manual type estates up and down the country.

Spiritually dead houses can be bulldozed into contour relief ready for our new homes to look out on.

Among the parks, greens, and market gardens will run the heavy transport lines. We should leave to a graceful old age the tubes, roads and railways with their service stations, garages, sidings, goods yards, linking them where necessary to our new deck-served elements.

To plan the elaborate elevation or depression of heavy transport routes

[14] 1966. Gigantic machine in operation
1953/55 beside Thorpe Hall near Corby.

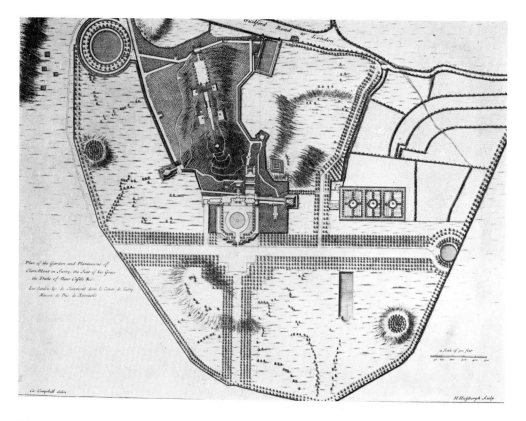

55. Parks, greens and market gardens: the three estates. 'Plan of the Garden and Plantations of Clare Mont in Surrey, the Seat of his Grace the Duke of New Castle &c.' – from Campbell's *Vitruvius Britannicus*

is unreal. In ten or twenty years we may be as far ahead again as the 1950's are in advance of the 1910's: already we can fly to Edinburgh cheaper than 1st Class rail.

When towns contract the clearing ground may make possible the long desired direct and simple motor routes and junctions which orientate the city, making obvious its relationship with its region. Rivers, docks, canals and estuaries, no longer ill-appointed and enmeshed in a decayed property/street jungle, will become part of the urban landscape that all will ultimately share. The great ships and cranes, the continuous motion and change of the waterways will enter the life of the great city.

GROUND LEVEL	DECK LEVEL
Parks, greens, and market gardens	Those things that are necessary to the life of the street.
Horizontal industry	Workshops, clinics, hotels, chapels, public gardens, office buildings etc.
Places of assembly and ceremonial	

GROUND LEVEL	DECK LEVEL
Road — service stations transit storage	Street — all pedestrians hand vehicles
Rail — stations sidings goods yards	Space — new lifts
Air — major airfields	Air — helicopters hoppycopters
Water — rivers, canals, estuaries, docks	

56. Edinburgh from the castle 1824

57–60. Only contour relief is bold enough to tell from above.

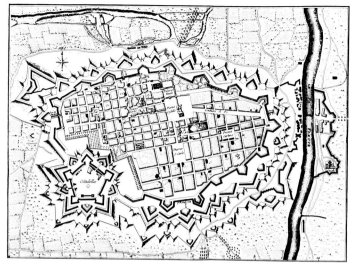

57. Plan of old Turin

58. Ineradicable marks. Fyfield Down, Wiltshire; air view of Celtic field system

72

59. Maiden Castle, Dorset, from the air. An Iron Age hill fort, overlying a Neolithic camp. Foundations of a small Romano–British temple within the fortifications

60. Castle Rising, Norfolk, by a Sicilian Norman architect

73

5 The nature of home; its equipment and furniture

When homes re-enter the city, the ratio of people coming from afar and those 'from around the corner' will be inverted; and as a result the problem of coping with the vast crowds who travel will be greatly diminished.

The city will resolve itself into fully identified Quarters: people associated with offices could, if they chose, live near offices; those with factories near factories; those with communications near communications. The reverse of what happens now, when even those who might wish to

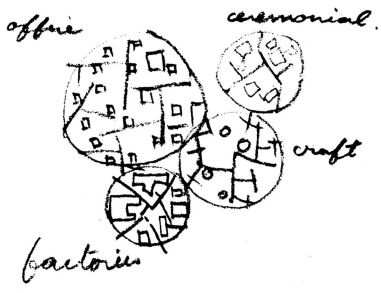

61. Golden Lane study. Fully identified quarters

live near their work are forced into a commuting pattern, finding a place to lay their heads where they may. Our aim is to provide free choice. The opportunity for living and working in proximity, in harmony. (That for some such a harmony may require physical separation of home and work does not affect the basic idea; for even a dormitory suburb is in fact 'a fully identified Quarter'.) The hope is that the advantages of close physical association will draw people to the clearly different districts of the city – cause an urban revival – a new city in which the home will be very much the centre of all activities.

62. Nothing is more ordered than a bachelor's apartment. *S. Jerome in his study*, by Antonello da Messina

It becomes immediately obvious when we try to draw the first perspective of a furnished interior of a new kind of dwelling, that the whole easily attainable world of furniture, objects and equipment is not in the same spirit as the way of life we are trying to project.

Once this doubt is there, the thing you can buy appears obsolete.

A new pattern of association and a new dwelling mean a new way of looking at objects and possessions.

This will require an enormous effort, for we are products of the school system, and our lives reflect the docility of our acceptance. For most people there is no refusing those set pieces on four legs that are as statutory for suburban decency as wedding rings.

With eyes given us by the photographer we see life stopped for us: the second of living that sums us up. Or more slowly, the Victorian plate camera portraits of the breathing, the living, sitter. We must cultivate a sense of awareness, of whereabouts in time; to be of the previous age is to be of the dark ages. No age is so primitive as the one immediately past, none so out of step, so out of consonance with our own.

The supreme monument to the home made possible entirely by availability – increased transportation and manufacturing – is the Victorian interior: fire irons, art works, brasses, vases, table mats, odd tables, more chairs, trophies; all go in.

America still has this kind of goods-economy where sewing machines can be huge cabinets, and refrigerators hold enough for a family and a horse to withstand a lengthy siege; symbols of property, as was the wardrobe in its day. Symbols of property seem unmodern.

More and more fixtures are being included in the house. They spread out from the kitchen till the house is totally cupboarded and shelved, tenants entombed by fitments like Tutankhamun.

As architects it is the act of living that interests us – how we live – and furniture and how we dispose it are only appurtenances of this act of living.

For the calm future even our objects of everyday use should be as unpretentious as possible, the chair chair, the table table, and the cup cup.

The possession of inviolable space is the individual's basic NECESSITY.

As tempo quickens . . . amenities must increase
as territorial assets diminish . . . convenience must replace

There must be,

insulation	against noise
air conditioning	,, dirt
Garché rubbish converter	,, waste accumulation
w.c. self-digestion system	,, ,,

central heating	against	waste accumulation
refrigerator	,,	lack of space
dryers	,,	,,
washing machines	,,	,,
usable extra space	,,	lack of outdoor space
ease of communication	,,	lack of country
sky – verdure	,,	,,
height (view)	,,	lack of scenic background
smokeless city	,,	lack of country air
district identification	,,	lack of atmosphere

Le Corbusier's Unité is a rack as for wine bottles, topped by a tray of individual 'objects', ventilators, surface activities. As ever with Le Corbusier, this building has in it the seeds of what we want to do.

63. Le Corbusier's wine-rack. 'The world's most ingenious architect has a new idea. Many architects are still groping towards notions le Corbusier had twenty years ago. Now he has a new idea. "Prefab. flats dropped into a steel frame like bottles into a rack." ' – from *Picture Post*, July 2, 1949

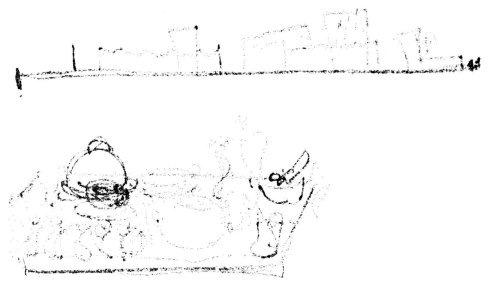

64. Tea-tray diagram. The familiar English tea tray on which objects are arranged has a single function in unity; diverse parts serve an end

In readiness for high-density solutions we have explored the small separate house,[15] evolving a four point house:

1. parents' unit
2. children's unit
3. eating and preparations
4. family extra, be it pigeon cote, sun parlour or Grandma's bedsit.

With this as our basis we attempt to give volumetric identity to each unit.

The parts of the house, although diverse, add up to 'home' which is:
aedicule
a roof over one's head
shelter.

We instinctively dislike the flat roof because it does not carry out visually this sheltering function. The home of man when primarily shelter, however transitory or mobile, always appears to cover. Nomads prefer the upturned bowl, cup, saucer, cap, hat; encircling as well as covering. Only when certain aspects of exposure are required – sleeping out, drying produce – does man naturally make his roof flat, as an outside room.

[15] 1966. In England in 1953 building licences were given on application for 1000 sq. ft. area houses.

78

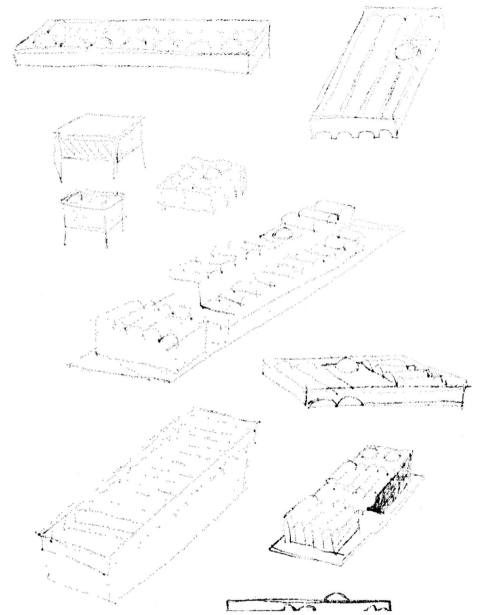

65. Tray houses

The 'box-frame', the rack into which our dwellings are slotted: the structural bridge on which a variety of dwellings are placed like conserves on a shelf: in different ways both are constricting. We need a structural idea for our multi-level dwellings as flexible and natural-seeming in approach as the dragonfly on a rush stalk.

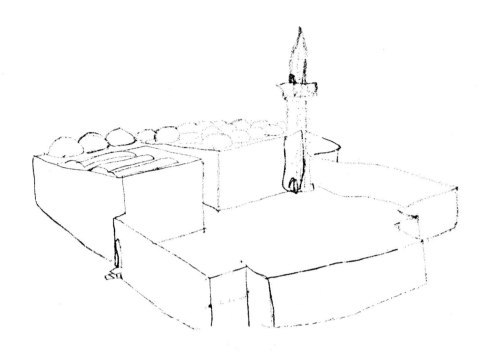

66, 67, Mosque, Houmt Souk, Djerba

6 The Great Society

Up and down the City road
In and out the Eagle
That's the way the money goes:
so said the philosopher of the first trek to work. But today's buyer of the
early morning ticket may have no energy to philosophise. Dull acceptance
on his part; but in the world, by some mysterious telepathy, the same idea
germinates spontaneously at the same time, and people begin to think
again of human associations: that from the conflicts and contradictions of
modern society we can build epic cities.

Whole levels of association are missed in our mechanically democratic
society.

The old houses in the depressed areas might be said to have 'their
hands soiled'. They have a hard-earned place, a character, a geographic
reality; our roots.

The housing estates are a no-man's-land of no particular occupation or
calling, where talk from door to door or across the street is incongruous,
and control of children impossible. Houses are too widely and illogically
placed for group observations or checking of would-be misdoers. Gangs
form, destruction takes place, municipal trees and grass are killed, no-one
feels responsible; there is no body of parental opinion.

The same is true of flatted development where the tarmac ground is
equally barren of spirit and social responsibility. 'Shouting down'
becomes a greater nuisance to the neighbours than anything created by the
gangs out of sight and out of mind.[16]

Delinquency thrives in families not in meaningful association with
society.

[16] 1966. Woodberry Down, a show estate of the L.C.C. in the early fifties, is already beaten to a slum by tenants incapable of the concept of 'holding in trust' for those following after. It would seem that state education has been wrongly orientated for these people.

The prevention officer is no substitute for the subtler pressure by human association, and the new Welfare process of care becomes degrading for all concerned.

Prisons – containers for criminals – demean and sap society. 'Replanting' the criminal, to make his own society with others – building it up again from a primitive level – on a Pacific or useless island, might create new patterns of association.

Ahead is a change in society as radical as the change of work-home relationship brought about by the industrial revolution.

Thousands build an oil refinery – a few men run it.

Huge machine shops – a few overseers.

Atomic plant and power – a few watchers.

No manual workers?

No heavy industry?

It is possible that with the advent of atomic power, automation and so on, our 'workers' will return for physical pleasure to the land, back to the crofts, reclaiming the moors, back to Soay, the outer Hebrides and the abandoned Scottish islands. It is as easy to sit in a Cumberland farm kitchen watching TV as in a Surbiton one – and less interference from cars out on the fells.

We must welcome changing patterns of association; be content to follow on swiftly, smoothly, as naturally as we can. The 'tools' given into our hands were developed to fit the problems right up to the minute they pass to our care – we are as relay runners. We lumber ourselves if we resist the possibilities offered for our future. Only by making assumptions, guessing ahead, can we supply homes even for the present. It will be necessary that we teach and learn at the same time, how to inhabit and what the habitat should be.

If we are ever to take this decisive step to build ahead of what is currently acceptable, there must be a reality in which to work. Housing subsidies[17] come between us and the individual's choice. There can only be a reality where the individual makes a choice from given and real alternatives.

Houses or guns

guns or butter

[17] 1968. Actual figures are hard to come by, but this news item gives some indication of the situation. The subsidised rent is between one third and one half of the economic rent. 'The GLC's most surprising tenant is living for a few weeks at the top of the East End's tallest block of flats. The tenant – Ernö Goldfinger, the architect who designed the block – has moved into one of the 26-storey flats at Rowlett Street, Poplar . . . He pays approximately £11 10s a week rent, exclusive of rates but including central heating. (This is the cost without any subsidy from the ratepayer or taxpayer. The subsidised rent for the flat will be £4 15s 6d, including heating, but exclusive of rates). Mr Goldfinger and his wife have four rooms plus kitchen and bathroom . . .' – *Architectural Design*, March 1968.

TV or picture window
car or sun lounge
clothes or model home.

Subsidies make our tackling of the problem of the house and the house-group unreal, and the choice of the individual a spurious one. Averages and Gallup polls on acceptability become increasingly based on a shadow.

A mechanical democratic society is one in which the individual has no say in how his money is to be spent for society's good. How we live, what kind of people as a community we are: in these great decisions we have no voice.

Just as the human association pattern in the depressed areas is clear, so the part that each plays

breadwinner
home manager - life mechanic
next generation
last generation   is clearly understood.

Of these the new pair is the star turn,

each star has its ascendance
and its wane.

We must cater ahead, always ahead of this new pair.

The house must be directed towards the requirements of the pair, not by some misconception of the rights of man where everybody is owed a minimum bourgeois standard, whether they wish it or not. (The pair needs only a cell for itself and a cell for its car, and must not be presented with a semi-detached house simply because the previous generation bourgeois had such a house.)

The pair needs only a cell plus, given at once.
After that it is the individual's own decision.

open space
enclosed space
extra cells (as distinct from space)
fine finishes and fittings   equipment
the bare necessities   better car
bare structure   better clothes

The choice should be the individual's not the State's.

83

7 The stuff and decoration of the urban scene

The Heroic Period of modern architecture finished in 1929, and work subsequent to this can be regarded as exploratory for the second great creative period beginning now. Both periods are characterised by simultaneous parallel development in architecture, engineering, painting and sculpture; the attitudes, theorems and images of each finding unsought consonances in the others.

It was inevitable that the International Style which evolved out of this Heroic Period, and which derived much of its invention from the reduction of problems to their basic elements and relationships, should lose its dynamic when most of the problems had been thus explored. For after all, when the basic kitchen has been achieved what can possibly follow?

Only Dada followed another road which we have taken twenty years to rediscover.

The cult of simplicity does not necessarily produce order, and as problems grew larger the simple surfaces and volumes became vacuums into which applied neo-plasticist ornament (Royal Festival Hall, London), and technique (U.N.O., New York) were sucked.

The position can be stated thus. In the twenties a work of art or a piece of architecture was a finite composition of simple elements, elements which have no separate identity but exist only in relation to the whole; the problem of the fifties is to retain the clarity of intention of the whole but to give the parts their own internal disciplines and complexities. This kind of ordering, as opposed to geometric ordering, must be the basis of all creative endeavour from the city to the object.

The concept of society should be one of motion and change not stasis, and plastically this should be apparent.

People and objects in motion and change are both the stuff and the decoration of the urban scene.

84

68. Jackson Pollock at work

In 1949 at Peggy Guggenheim's palazzo in Venice we saw the first manifestation of the new ordering, in the painting of Jackson Pollock.

In a roomful of academic abstract painting Pollock seemed too good to be true: the ghost of the twenties had at last been laid and the way was clear.

At last we were free from the shadow of our international grandfathers, free to solve our problems in our own way.

The painting of Jackson Pollock is a different sort from any that we had ever seen before. It is more like a natural phenomenon, a manifestation rather than an artifact; complex, timeless, n-dimensional and multi-vocative.

Comparable developments have taken place in structural design, in which the actual behaviour and the properties of the materials are more accurately accounted for. This has led, as in art, to the consideration of the parts not as simply acting, but as things in themselves with their own internal disciplines complexly acting in a total system of forces.

In Le Corbusier's book on his Unité d'Habitation at Marseilles there is one very significant page which shows the plan of St Dié and a student sketch of the Carthusian monastery of Ema in Tuscany. Of this sketch Corbu says: 'L'organisation harmonieuse du phénomène collectif et du phénomène individuel, y est résolue dans la sérénité, la joie et l'efficience.'

69. Eduardo Paolozzi. Sculpture from 'This is Tomorrow' 1956

70. Eduardo Paolozzi, *Man's Head* 1954

71. Jean Dubuffet, *Dématérialisation*; ink drawing 1952

No-one can doubt the validity (in the middle ages) of the monastic system, or fail to be moved by the serenity of the plastic resolution – for resolution of relationships *is* architecture. But the assurance and clarity of St Dié[18] rest on an invalid relationship between the individual and the collective.

Families do not now (nor did they in the fifteenth century) live an introspective scholastic life where the only relationship that matters is that of God and Man. That was the life at Ema, and Ema is the seed from which Unité and St Dié have grown.

In Unité seen negatively the out-turned cell faces impersonal sun and space. Man scurries along from Victorian lifts down gloomy corridors to the solitary confinement of his private drawer.

[18] 1966. Yet it is indisputable that the unbuilt plan for St Dié contained more of value than all the ghastly new town areas the French have built.

72. Victor Pasmore. Detail of a mural for a restaurant, Festival of Britain 1951

73. Comet 1952; the world's first civil jet airliner. 'Beneath his feet opens a cooling duct to the cabin pressurisation and air-conditioning system. To the left an engine-bay ventilator. Inside, the turbine-driven compressor which snatches air screaming through the intake, feeds it to the kerosene combustion-expansion chamber – where the "jet" begins.' – *Picture Post* caption, 17 May 1952. What religious sect can rival this for intoning while watching its rites?

Nevertheless it is the most significant building of our time, existing in space but outside time, like the Temple of Poseidon at Paestum.

It is the life-work of a man whose whole life has been devoted to architecture in its grandest sense, and it embodies the whole of the Corbusier doctrine in its purest form.

It proves beyond all doubt that the vertical openly spaced green city is possible and can provide a way of life in many respects superior to that provided in the best horizontal garden city. Privacy is assured, sun penetrates, balconies make family life possible, shops are not far away, mechanical equipment is excellent, the view is superb and will remain superb, as will the acres of surrounding garden.[19] All this is the result of an inventive, an exploratory, social attitude, a remembering of the idea that a city (even a miniature city) is to cater for the fundamental human needs.

In the Unité for the first time we have a modern building of inch by inch interest, a building that grows greater in time and does not storm the eye and leave the heart unmoved. The factory-made parts, the pre-cast elements, the patterns of shuttering are arranged with consummate skill for ends new to modern architecture.

Order is the end of all human activity.
Order and simplicity are not synonymous.
Parts must be things in themselves.

Flexibility and identity are the logical results of a proper attitude towards 'the part'.

Alvar Aalto tells how after the war when the problem of rebuilding Finland was desperately urgent, building elements were studied with a view to their standardisation. The best timber was to be exported, and that which remained was cut into scantlings of various standard sizes. With these the designs for the houses were prepared. For windows, doors, etc., a small number of standard heights and widths were adopted which were to be combined to give many sizes and proportions. A standard hinge was produced to replace the dozens previously used for different jobs. A standard stair tread was designed to fit varying floor to floor heights by a simple sliding action of tread over tread – the tread to riser relationship remaining a constant – following a natural law.

In the rest of Europe another route was followed: the industrialisation of the building industry so ardently advocated by Le Corbusier in the

[19] 1966. Both the Unité idea and its garden have since been compromised by other buildings too close and too high. The urban idea can now only be seen in the plans for St Dié.

74. Ema. Le Corbusier drawing from *Unité d'Habitation de Marseille* 1950

twenties became a partial reality by the late forties. Unfortunately those firms with capital enough to make the fundamental changes needed inherited the outlook and techniques of old-style large-unit line production.

75. Mount Grace Priory, Yorkshire. Carthusian

For example, in England immediately after the war a programme of prefabrication of whole houses, schools, etc., was initiated. At least twenty firms produced complete houses, in steel, aluminium or concrete which made obligatory the cottage life of the late middle ages (with all mod. con. of course). Similarly, schools perpetuated the pattern of inter-war education theory. Local authorities quickly realised the limited applications of such buildings (which cost as much or more than those constructed by traditional hand methods) and production stopped. But the attitude that made them possible is still prevalent throughout the industry. Whole bathrooms, kitchens, cupboards, storage assemblies, gas and electrical cookers, sinks, drainers, etc., are produced by dozens of firms; each thing being individually standard and self-sufficient, but incapable of combining with and completing any larger complex.

In an attempt to bring about some sort of ordering many manu-facturers have voluntarily complied with certain standard dimensions (e.g. the 1' 9" kitchen module) and dozens of working parties and

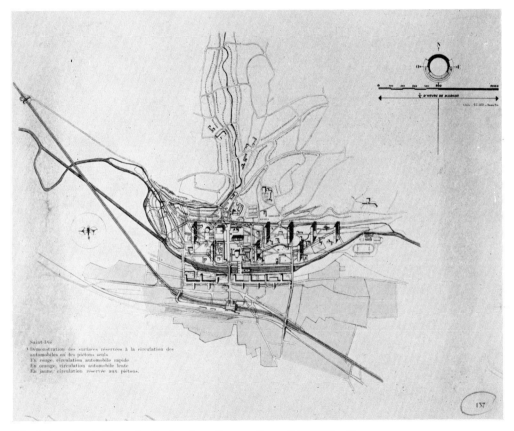

76. Sainte-Dié. From le Corbusier, *Oeuvre Complète 1938–46*

77. Le Corbusier's *Unité* on the Boulevard Michelet, Marseilles, as originally conceived. Photographed in 1950. A building in a landscape, this is le Corbusier's 43-year-old dream from Ema realised

committees have worked on the problem of dimensional co-ordination. Dimensional co-ordination is an attempt to produce a series of standard dimensions which can be used singly, repetitively or additively for building. The basic 'human derived' dimension in German, English and

78. *Unité*, detail

79. Paestum

American systems is 3′ 4″, with related dimensions from the Fibonacci series – 8″, 16″, 24″, 40″, 64″, etc., or 'preferred' dimensions – 8″, 1′ 4″, 2′ 2″, 2′ 8″, 3′ 4″, etc. (Le Corbusier's Modulor is based on 6′ 0″ – height of English detective story hero – and related dimensions on the 'section d'or'.)

In all these systems an extremely arbitrary dimension is made the basis of a rigorous mathematical series. This is an advanced form of self-delusion and can lead to space-blindness.

Furthermore, the control of space by dimensional series involves the use of those same dimensions for whatever materials define that space.

80. Hunstanton, Norfolk, under construction 1952

This means inevitably that dimensions are given to structure and finish purely for the sake of the system, and not because the structure or finish is operating at its best with those dimensions.

In fact we are getting conditions exactly opposite to those intended by those who put forward aesthetic and moral arguments for the use of dimensional systems; for the observed consonances in nature on which the validity of these systems depend grow out of circumstance and performance and are not due to any imposed laws.

The parts must operate according to their own laws. Only in this way can true consonance be attained. The consonances found in the mediaeval town – street, walls, houses, vehicles, furniture, people – are due to the operation of this law, and this is the law that must govern the creation of our cities.

Dimensional co-ordination *as a mystique* is a piece of mumbo-jumbo, the result of a misconception of the role of mechanisation in building.

In any complex the part must obey its own laws. Obedience to their internal disciplines by all the parts will ensure the harmony of the whole; the city being a symphony of many such harmonies.

Thus the house, the street, the district and ultimately the city, are defined and find plastic resolution. Order is obvious in the family likeness of part to part.

Except in the smallest elements (e.g. nails, hinges) disciplines of absolute standardisation are unnecessary. Mathematically derived proportion is a confidence trick.

In the part is the whole.

81. Sutton Coldfield television mast 1949

8 Realisation: cost, legislation, versus dreams

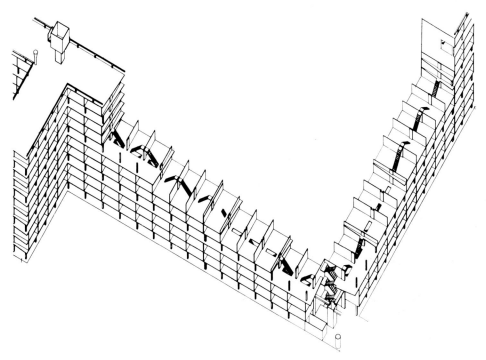

82. Golden Lane study, construction

The Golden Lane Project was a pilot scheme to try and develop solutions and techniques. Suppose we project a scheme to optimum social and structural standards?

The houses would be larger and simpler than those in Golden Lane, where rooms and equipment were provided to statutory (and obsolete) standards.

Internal finishes, partitioning, equipment and services would in the first place be of the simplest. We would provide enough space to make civilised life possible, and occupiers would furnish those things which were personally essential. Thus we could provide for the man who would die without a Morris wallpaper or a private bathroom for guests.

For the 'cobbler or the candlestick-maker',[20] his work-bench and store could be right at his door; no need to travel from Hendon to Holborn.

83. Cobbler's stall 1760

To build up street and district complexes at several levels with such houses a structural system capable of absorbing considerable variation must be devised, one that can give the varying lengths of decks, different kinds of district arrangements, and such links and penetrations as will ensure the ease of circulation and looseness of grouping that is fundamental to the idea. And the system must be economical, capable of competing with other forms of city arrangement on their own terms.

As we have seen the maximum height for residential development seems to be between 150 and 200 feet. At such heights the logical structural form would seem to be the box-frame, which is economical up to about 16 normal floors or 160 feet.

[20] 1966. In larger enterprises the problems of servicing are in conflict with housing.

84. Golden Lane study; four deck version

A typical complex would have five levels of decks.

The position of thoroughfares – the main routes – and the general location of shops, markets, banks, small workshops, etc., would have to be decided before the streets-in-the-air are established.

Within one generation the city could serve us again, if we could only make a start. And with a flexible city notion (not tied to finite scale or number) we can cope with the inevitable changes.

In the past hill-towns like Mistra were abandoned when the descent to the fields to labour, and ascent to sleep at night, became no longer a matter of life or death; when a man could with safety dwell by his fields.

As soon as we can offer a suitable alternative to the semi and small plot we can expect to see the suburbs abandoned for a better way of life.

The idea of an opened-up, pedestrian-decked lived-in city

    is completely possible,
    is capable of organisation,
    is not limited to the work of one man or a time schedule or a style.

The idea can be simply stated.

It is an idea capable of extension. Its deployment is not dependent on geometric rigour, and sections can be built as sites become available, and

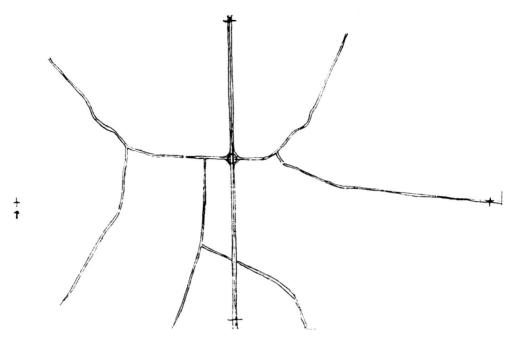

85. Roads on the ground. The Golden Lane overlay

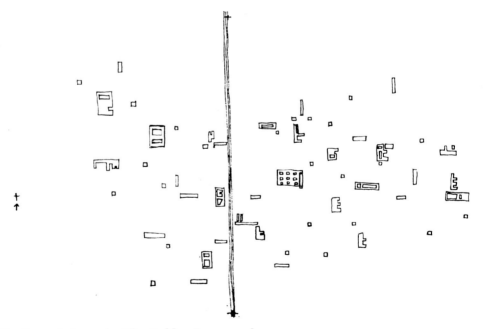

86. Ground elements. The Golden Lane overlay

98

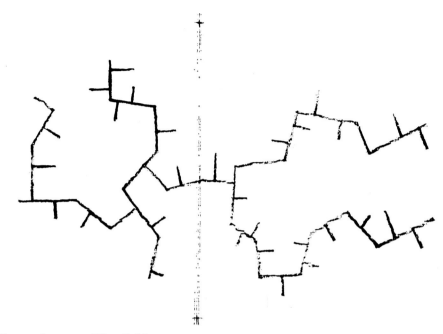

87. Space elements. The Golden Lane overlay

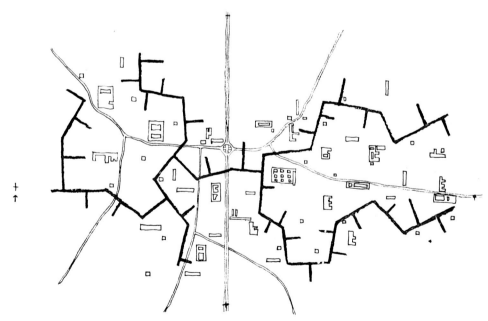

88. The Golden Lane complete overlay

99

linked up later. This action could gradually free the decayed belt which is around almost all our cities. Applied to London the old domestic fringe – Soho, Holloway and Bethnal Green – would form a renewed edge to the Inner City. Those elements outermost would form battlements from which one would look over the cleared area to the foothills of Highgate and Hampstead.

The West City would have its Finchley, St John's Wood, Paddington and Shepherds Bush re-defined and re-orientated about it.

By this time small units would be emerging from the sea of outer suburbs – forms growing finite in their leisure fields.

This process is applicable to all old urban areas. To suggest but one example, how many derelict lots on the banks of the lower Tyne could provide magnificent sites for homes like those in Le Corbusier's 'Deux viaducs' or his 'Maison Locative' at Algiers?[21]

Every city would be able to feel its form; see the land roll about it.

The man in the street would see the city landmarks that at every move spear him into exact relationship with his surroundings.

No longer would city contours go unnoticed and famous buildings be tucked away: like Istanbul we should see our city swing about us in ever changing meaningful patterns.

89. Istanbul. Sketch by le Corbusier from *The City of Tomorrow* (*Apropos d'Urbanisme*)

[21] See illustration 90.

100

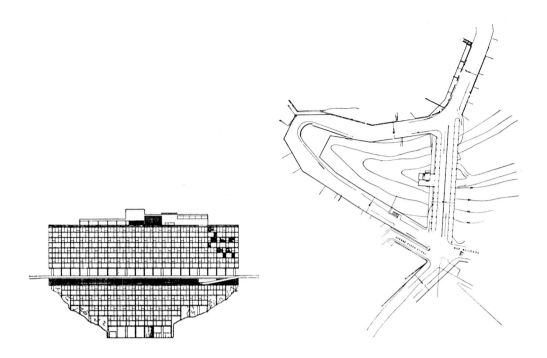

90. Le Corbusier's scheme for two viaducts in Algiers, 1933. (Above) Various levels in elevation; ground level garage, motor road. (Below) Sections of proposed treatment of hillside streets. From *Oeuvre Complète 1929–34*

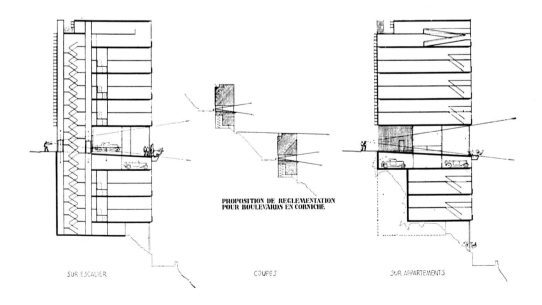

PROPOSITION DE REGLEMENTATION
POUR BOULEVARDS EN CORNICHE

SUR ESCALIER   COUPES   SUR APPARTEMENTS

Essays on urban theory

Between early 1953, when the Urban Re-identification *document was finished, and 1955, when the first of the urban theory essays was published, occurred the for us momentous 9th Congress of CIAM at Aix-en-Provence (July 1953).*

In Urban Re-identification *we were in a sense writing in the dark; after Aix, we had seen the masters (even Léger made an appearance), experienced the Unité inaugurated in triumph, and sensed-out those of our own generation who were on our waveband.*

On the panels we nailed up at Aix were diagrams, photographs and descriptions from the just-finished 'UR' document. Nailed up, these were subject to the scrutiny of one's equals. So began the family dialogues of Team 10.

To the conversions and conversations of Aix, and to the attempts in the months that followed to put down on paper that sense of new beginning felt there, are due both the greater depth and the more direct nature – 'this is what we must do in this situation' – of all the essays in the second part of this book.

The first essay is really a summary of the 'UR' document in which the evidence of the new thinking and the new aesthetic is shown in real buildings for the first time.

By 1955 we had completed our first real building, the Hunstanton school; we had submitted and had had rejected our Coventry Cathedral and Sheffield University competition projects; and we had begun to realise that in the ordinariness and quiet of our Golden Lane project – its innocence of style – we had achieved the nearest thing to a personal style. In a sense we had begun the great walk back.

9 The built world: Urban re-identification[22]

Each generation feels a new dissatisfaction, and conceives of a new idea of order.

This is architecture.

Young architects today feel a monumental dissatisfaction with the buildings they see going up around them.

For them, the housing estates, the social centres and the blocks of flats are meaningless and irrelevant. They feel that the majority of architects have lost contact with reality and are building yesterday's dreams when the rest of us have woken up in today. They are dissatisfied with the ideas these buildings represent, the ideas of the Garden City Movement and the Rationalism of the thirties.

These two movements achieved their built form by discovering the aesthetic means to achieving a social programme.

The Garden City Movement is social in origin; Ebenezer Howard saw in the idea of combining town and country, a 'Peaceful Path to Real Reform'.

The image left in the mind by his book is one of a railway architecture for clean but bewildered working men.

The Garden City idea was Ebenezer Howard's, but its form came from Camillo Sitte, who was the first to study mediaeval towns as deliberate arrangements – as compositions. After Camillo Sitte common-sense order and expression were to give way to picturesque composition. The garden cities as realised owe more to the misunderstanding of the mediaeval town than to the reforming drive of the railway age.

From the garden cities has come forty years of town planning legislation. They have fixed the density structure, the pattern of garden and house, and the aimless road system of our new council housing

[22] First published *Architectural Design*, June 1955.

91. Crawley New Town, Sussex, 1951. The roots of our dissatisfaction

estates. They have perpetuated to this day the official opinion, in 1912, of what the deserving working man should have.

The Garden City Movement has mothered the New Towns. In them the concept of 'balanced social structure', and the careful provision of survey-assessed amenities, has reached its ultimate anti-climax.

In the more 'progressive' places, especially on the Continent, the Garden City tradition has given way to the Rationalism of the thirties.

The social driving force of this movement was slum clearance, the provision of sun, light, air and green space in the over-populated cities. This social content was perfectly matched by the form of functionalist architecture, the architecture of the academic period which followed the great period of Cubism and Dada and de Stijl, of the Esprit Nouveau.

105

This was the period of the minimum kitchen and the four functions, the mechanical concept of architecture.

Today in every city in Europe we can see Rational Architecture being built. Multi-storey flats running north-south in parallel blocks just that distance apart that permits winter sun to enter bottom storeys, and just high enough to get fully economic density occupation of the ground area. Where the extent of development is sufficient we can see the working out of the theoretical isolates, dwelling, working, recreation (of body and spirit), circulation; and we wonder how anyone could possibly believe that in this lay the secret of town building.

The dissatisfaction we feel today is due to the inadequacy of either of these movements to provide an environment which gives form to our generation's idea of order. The historical built forms were not arrived at

92. Tiree, Argyll; house in crofting village. The structure of towns: the dwelling, the community

106

by chance or Art, they achieved order through significant organisation, and the forms have a permanent validity, a secret life, which outlives their direct usefulness. Each one of us recognises the Street, the Place, the Village Green, the Grand Boulevard, the Kraal, or the Bidonville, as urban inventions, as extensions of the house and components of the town which satisfied the needs and aspirations of past generations in other places.

Why is it we cannot find for each place the form for our generation? We are members of a non-demonstrative society. We no longer cluster at the well, meet at the market place, dance on the village green, get milk from the farm, visit to get information, or journey to inform. Into our houses is brought light, heat, water, entertainment, information, food,

93. Hydra, Greece. The structure of towns: houses that are variations from an archetype, not identical units. Aggregation (not repetition) of the dwelling – the community

107

94. House at Ronchamp by le Corbusier, 1954. Evidence of a new way of thinking: aesthetics

etc. We are no longer forced by our physical needs into the old patterns of association. Surely we must be mad to keep on building forms evolved in previous cultures with their own unique associational patterns, and expect them to work – or even more important – to make us feel connected?

In England the key problem is that of the council house.

A form must be found for the house which is capable of being put together with others of a similar sort, so as to form bigger and equally comprehensible elements which can be added to existing villages and towns in such a way as to revitalise the traditional hierarchies, and not destroy them. The relationship of the country and the town, the bank and the house, the school and the pub, is conveyed by the form they take. Each form is an active force, it creates the community, it is life itself made manifest. Today we have a literate society. We are involved in mass housing not as reformers but as form givers. We must evolve an architecture from the fabric of life itself, an equivalent for the complexity of our way of thought, our passion for the natural world and our belief in the nobility of man.

In a rough and ready way we have made a start – a 'doorstep philosophy' – an ecological approach to the problem of habitat – and a new aesthetic.

95. Steps up into town core at Säynatsälo by Alvar Aalto. Evidence of a new way of thinking: town pattern

The series of Unités d'Habitation of Le Corbusier (the first achieved in the teeth of fanatical opposition) and his house and hostel at the chapel of Ronchamp are evidence enough of a new way of thinking.

Alvar Aalto has built an extension to a village in which he has established a new pattern for the relationship between the individual and the collective, without resorting to traditional street forms; a new complexity which has little to do with the cosy sentimentality of Scandinavia which it superficially resembles. And at the 9th Congress of CIAM at Aix-en-Provence, projects were presented from Morocco, Holland and England which showed a simultaneous emergence of the forms of a new way of thinking. Of these projects, one, collective housing for Arabs at Casablanca by the architects of ATBAT (Atelier de Batisseurs), has since been realised. In this scheme the Arab way of life has achieved in an urban environment, through twentieth century technological means, the unity and brilliance of an Atlas village without being in any way sentimental or revivalist.

These buildings and projects are evidence that an architecture of here

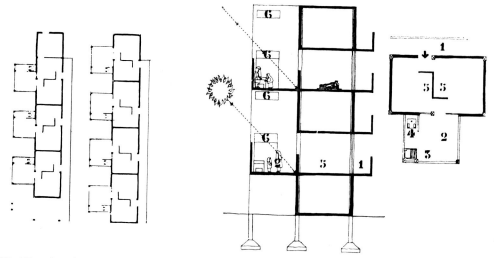

96. Housing in Morocco by Atbat. (*a*) alternate floor plans showing staggered patios. (*b*) typical section and plan. Key: 1, access balcony. 2, patio. 3, hearth. 4, WC. 5, room. 6, breezeway (on section only). The structure of towns: basic units

97. Morocco City Unité by Atbat. The new blocks compared with the unimaginative sprawl of official rehousing in the rear. The structure of towns: town pattern

and now is possible, and they provide a composite image which may help to make clearer the exposition of the ideas that lie behind them.

Firstly the 'doorstep philosophy'.

To take our own situation, it seems not unreasonable to question the suitability of, for example, Housing Manual type houses and layouts, for every county, every type of community, and every variation of climate. Surely the pattern of a mining village in County Durham and an out-county estate of the London County Council should reflect in some way the life pressures and aspirations of the inhabitants. Yet, as one travels about England, can one honestly see any real differences? Perhaps this is a reflection of the Welfare State; that we want nothing more. But is this true? It is perhaps more true that no alternatives have been presented, that no choice has been offered. Few architects live in the housing estates they build. Let us therefore start our thinking from the moment the man or child steps outside his dwelling. Here our responsibility starts, for the individual has not got the control over his extended environment that he has over his house, which can become palace or pig-sty irrespective of what is provided in the first place.

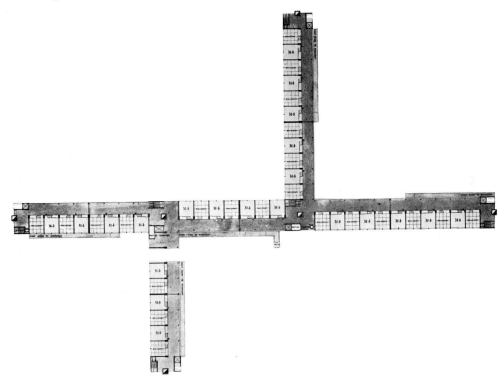

98. Plan of a deck with yard gardens, in the Golden Lane project. The structure of towns: basic units – house with garden – decks – streets in the air

We must try and find out in what way this basic contact should take place, how many houses should be put together, what their shared facilities should be – the equivalent to the village pump; continually questioning the arbitrariness of existing solutions.

This is the basic step of the ecological approach to the problem of habitat: the house is a particular house in a particular place, part of an existing community, and it should try to extend the laws and disciplines of that community. In the Unité d'Habitation at Marseilles Le Corbusier has almost fallen over backwards trying to establish a definite relationship between the 'individual and the collective'. Thirty years ago he visited the Carthusian Monastery of Ema in Tuscany, and noted the extraordinary unity of organisation, which preserved the individual in seclusion while giving expression to the communal life and faith of the Order.

The Unité achieves just such a clarity.

The dwelling is a miniature Unité with a double height 'collective' space, and links through the balconies with the world outside.

The interior street provides an enclosed world of neighbours. The

99. The Golden Lane idea superimposed on an area of bombed Coventry. The structure of towns: town pattern – the decks joined together

shopping arcade and roof space belong to and give expression to the total community.

The pilotis are symbols of the participation of the Unité in the life of Marseilles and the surrounding countryside.

Up to now most architects have evaded the issue of the dialogue between the whole community and the piece that is being added, and have built imitation market-towns both inside and around our great cities, denying them the right to be urban forms (conversely, to suggest elaborate multi-level solutions for small places is absurd, for no-one wants to lose touch with the earth if he can avoid it).

And finally the new aesthetic.

There are in fragments already achieved the seeds of a new aesthetic.

The magnificent, intensely intellectual architecture of the twenties, the architecture of lyrical, polychromatic geometry, showed no interest in materials as such.

The new aesthetic starts again with life and with a love of materials. It tries to sum up the very nature of materials and the techniques with which they are put together, and, in an altogether natural way to establish a unity between the built form and the men using it.

It is strange that something as obvious, common and needed by all as the 'house' should have eluded our period. Prefabricated houses of the period just after the war seemed so nearly to miss the desired pattern; to be so near mass production, system building, and yet miss.[23]

The essay called Caravan: embryo appliance house?, *together with* Cluster Patterns *in which the thoughts behind the essay were demonstrated through illustrations of historical examples, were together an attempt to find by exploration what had been missed.*

10 Caravan: embryo appliance house?[24]

Cluster patterns

selected evocative illustrations with captions[25]

Probably no-one would deny that caravan sites are an eyesore, or that they tend to create conditions which administrators in England have striven to overcome by successive Byelaws and Health Acts. Nevertheless caravans

[23] It was obvious when the following essay was written that no-one wanted prefabricated houses. 'Housing' still remained a mystery. We were, and still are, only as near a solution as Le Corbusier showed us; and more often in rejecting his aesthetic, as far away in form as Adolph Loos. Until the best talent in the country is put on to housing, together with the capital resources now going for prototyping and developing rockets or fighting planes, there can be no answer at the scale at which the problem exists for society. Profits from housing (as there are hundreds of thousands to be built) are colossal and should pay for the talent required in big-scale operations. Only a perfected thing is worth multiplying.

[24] First published *Architectural Design*, September 1959.

[25] First published *Architect and Building News*, July 1956.

dumped in a casually offered field – on the increase all over the country – obviously provide a solution for a lot of people who want to opt out of the bye-law street or Garden City set-up. For some people the caravan provides a 'home' – with little or no outlay on furnishings – which is technological, twentieth century. Or there are people requiring, as it were, a permanent tent in the country. Or there are the childless, or the

100. Selim Bey's tent on Kara Deq, near Colemerik, Turkish Kurdistan. The magic of the desert camp

elderly couple whose children have left. Or there are the people who just naturally, together with a few hens, in any place, form Shacksville. In the caravan you see people as they might wish or dare to be; for the caravan is the nearest thing to an 'Appliance House' that the market has to offer. To get this much sense of freedom people in England are prepared to put up with conditions as primitive as those their great grandmothers knew: gimcrack sanitary arrangements, inadequate refuse disposal, mud outside the door, exposure to climate, lack of freehold.

115

101. Airstream Land Yacht in rocky scenery. Caravans properly used become objects in a more or less uninhabited landscape – not sub-standard dwellings

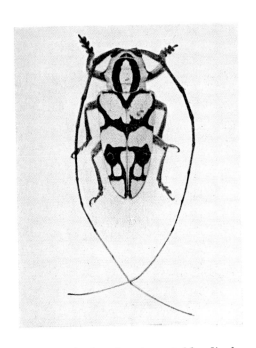

102. Exotic beetle. Acceptable display in a natural setting. Most caravans are totally unacceptable as objects in their display

103. Advertisement for Simoniz. Adman's dream world

104. Advertisement; car interior 1955. The caravan is as comfortable as the latest car model and, like the car, it represents a new freedom

Against the standard solution to the permanent dwelling the caravan is neat, like a big piece of equipment, has a place for everything like a well run office, has miniature appliances in scale with the spaces like a toy home, is as comfortable as this year's space-heated car. And like the car, the caravan represents a new freedom. It has become a sort of symbol as well as a sign of 'population in flux'. It has something of the cheerful, safe, transient feeling one gets driving along in a car.

105. Tents of the 33rd Infantry Regiment at Sebastopol, 1855. The old magic of a large camp site

106. 'Pair of brick bungalows suitable for midland counties' – from *Studio Year Book* 1919. A boiled-down, standardised version of the Garden City ideal

Young people who live in caravans are remote from the craftsman class of 1917 the Garden City was meant for. They are television watchers, buyers of leisure equipment, representing a new leisure, the results of education, the independent earning power of women, the new prosperity: expressing these forces in their aims and aspirations. A discriminating audience at a certain level, one that could and should be encouraged to steer clear forever of the semi-detached vortex of walnut bedroom suites with puckered pink eiderdown and puce china crinoline ladies. We as architects must recognise this desire potential, which they express as clearly as they know how through choice of what the market offers.

107. Life out of doors in paradise. By the Master of the Upper Rhine, *The Virgin Mary in the Garden of Paradise c.* 1410

108. Crofts near Staffin, northern Skye. Permanent buildings, natural answer

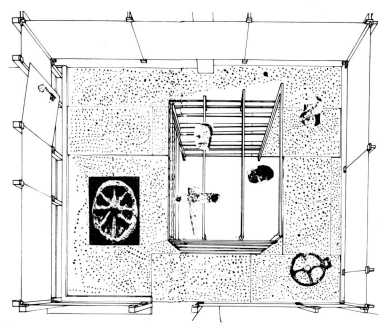

109. 'This is Tomorrow' Exhibition 1956; patio and pavilion. Fundamentals of human habitat; a piece of the world (patio), and an enclosed space (pavilion), furnished with symbols of human needs. (Collaboration by Nigel Henderson, Eduardo Paolozzi and the authors)

Equally, the caravan might conceal greater potential as a possible pointer to a new basic old people's cell, embodying and implying a new kind of retirement from the city. Snug and easy to clean.

110. 'House of the Future' 1956. Entrance door, hot air grilles, looking towards the patio garden

111. Projected mobile home park in Florida. This is what happens when caravanners start to put down roots. Rape of the idea of caravan, concreted in

When caravans are placed in any number on a site, however nicely or consciously, they fail to add up to anything more than a lot of different caravans. They offer no pointer whatever to the look of the new environment, any more than the outside of the caravan does the new architectural

112. Levittown, New York. Regimentation removes the magic from a housing estate

form for a living cell. But it is also precisely at these levels that ordinary housing most significantly fails. Thus comparison with permanent housing cannot redirect the caravan site. All that the caravan mania can do is make us re-examine the premises for all the expensive miles of estate roads, the acres of tiny 'gardens' all requiring fencing of some sort; and question whether the expense of collecting and allocating state subsidies to perpetuate the permanent brick house is worthwhile. Is this in fact what the new class of technologists (to take only one section of the community) really want? What house form, what kind of grouping, can we offer in exchange?

What is wanted in exchange?

What have the caravan dwellers got?

Or think they have got?

113. Wally Byam caravanners on the road to Guatemala

When the next essay was written in 1956 it was exactly ten years since the New Towns Act. The ideals of the New Towns' architects – neighbourhood planning and the picturesque layout – were by then realised on the ground, and elsewhere in the ten years 1946 to 1956 a whole new way of thinking had been evolving.

11 An alternative to the Garden City idea[26]

A town is by definition a specific pattern of association, a pattern unique for each group of people, in each location, at each time. To achieve this specific pattern the town must develop from principles which give the evolving organism consistency and unity.

Ideally a town plan is a statement of principles, and the realisation of the town should be in the hands of successive individual developers who, understanding the principles at every stage, assess what has gone before and by their activities each in turn mutate the whole. The construction of a New Town should start as a small *thing,* rather than on the scale of what is to come; each subsequent area should step up the scale. The whole would become in every way larger at each stage.

The first principle of town development should be:
Continuous objective analysis of the human structure and its change.

[26] Originated: 1954. Completed: 25.3.56. Finally revised: 30.3.56. Published *Architectural Design,* July 1956.

Such an analysis would include not only 'what happens', such as living in certain places, going to school, travelling to work and visiting shops, but also 'what motivates', the reasons for going to particular schools, choosing that type of work and visiting those particular shops. In other words, analysis would try to uncover a pattern of reality which includes human aspirations.

114. Robin Hood's Bay, Yorkshire, 1947.

The social data on which the New Towns are based accumulated during the war – all now obviously obsolete. Mass communications, change of manufacturing technology, and the increase in the standard of living, have produced an educated artisan class. The same forces have decreased the spending power of the upper middle classes, and their material aspirations now approximate to those of the new artisan technologist. The social structure to which the town planner has to give form is not only different but much more complex than ever before.

The various public services make the family more and more independent of actual physical contact with the rest of the community as individuals, and more turned in on itself.

Such factors would seem to make incomprehensible the continued acceptance of forms of dwellings and means of access which differ very little from those which satisfied the social reformers' dream before the first world war.

This is particularly so when one considers the increasing use of the motor car. It must be assumed that we will approach the American standard of mobility. A footpath off a windy ill-defined village green is a poor link between a heated car and a heated house.

Concerning the size and shape of community sub-division, it must first be recognised that in modern urban society there are no natural groupings above the level of the family. Furthermore, many recognisable social entities in existing settlements – say that of the street in a mining village – have been created by the built form. A valid social entity can result from architectural decisions. That is, decisions which include consideration of plastic organisation – the shape of the community.

The second principle of town development should be:
Establishing a positive relationship with the climate and the site.

For the design of buildings and layout of towns in tropical areas, it is an accepted method to establish the general principles of design by considering the ways in which the bad effects of the climate can be ameliorated, and its beneficial effects exploited.

To do this an analysis is made of sun angles and penetrations of rainfall, of wind directions, etc. The uses of sloping sites as wind traps, of vegetation as temperature control, etc., are also examined. The data thus obtained provide a discipline which can control the whole development.

A similar discipline clearly contributed to the clear pattern of settlement in the more rigorous parts of England. The isolated farmhouses of the Yorkshire moors have their blank backs to the worst exposure, for shelter is a practical and psychological necessity. And the narrow wynds of fishing villages, at right-angles to the wind sweeping up from the harbour mouth, deliberately exclude all sight and as much fury of the sea as possible.

In the gentler places where most people live, the forces of nature are not so obvious, but the worst aspects of climate are still open to amelioration and the beneficial ones to exploitation – the business of rain and cold for example.

In England it is rainy and cold for about eight months every year. This seems to call for houses that would both give, and look as if they gave, all-round protection. Double walls, double roofs, double windows, covered approaches, covered drying yards.

The English climate is not characterised by intense rain or cold but by changeability. The house, therefore, should be capable of grasping what fine weather it can get, grasping solar heat through south windows into the rooms and giving easy access to sheltered patios, roof gardens or terraces which can be arranged in a moment to catch the pleasures of our climate, and then closed up in a moment so that we can ignore it.

Such an attitude towards protection and changeability could guide the form of the whole layout.

For example, the normal present-day town centre is still based on the social and financial organisation of the middle ages, and its form derives from the great classic piazzas of northern Italy. But our climate would seem to demand that the circulation between such things as shops, places of entertainment, municipal offices, etc., should take place under cover. And if we have cars we want to be able to use them for just those things that take place at the centre.

The big hotel,[27] with its foyers, shops, restaurants, palm courts, etc., under centralised control and with adequate parking arrangements, is the prototype of this type of indoor centre.

The third principle of town development:
Extending and renewing the existing built complexes.

Any new development exists in a complex of old ones. It must revalidate, by modifying them, the forms of the old communities. The architect is no longer the social reformer but a technician in the field of form, who cannot rely on community centres, communal laundries, community rooms, etc., to camouflage the fact that the settlement as a whole is incomprehensible. Form is generated, in part by response to existing form, and in part by response to the Zeitgeist, which cannot be pre-planned. Every addition to a community, every change of circumstance, will generate a new response.

An aspect of this response is scale, the way in which the new part is organised plastically to give it meaning within the whole complex. As the complex changes with the addition of new parts, so the scale of the parts must change in order that they and the whole maintain a dynamic response.

What is being proposed here is an abolition of planning as we know it; the disappearance of the 'master-plan' and all detailed town-form planning. The procedure for developers would be, first, a thorough briefing as to the existing facts and the principles deduced from them.

[27] 1966. We are now very much concerned with the maintenance problems of big closed social spaces, and do not now regard the hotel as a suitable model.

Secondly, the individuals would assess the briefing and the form-demands of the existing built situation, and then get on with it. There should be no further controls.

Two generations ago Patrick Geddes pioneered survey techniques. His approach was that of the observer of organisms, and his analysis was concerned largely with improving the existing insanitary conditions. Today different compulsions are at work within us, our analysis has to be creative and not ameliorative. The end-product must be principles to guide a constructive urge, the principles of town building.

Le Corbusier's dream of a Ville Radieuse: the plans move us as little as the pattern on the paper table cloth at the Vieux Paris, which is indeed where it may have originated. How different are our reactions to the same image ! His sparking point excitement; ours, art-historical curiosity.
Yet the dream was real enough and is still relevant.

12 Cluster City – a new shape for the community[28]

'Here we have a promenade for pedestrians rising on a gentle ramp to first-floor level, which stretches before us as a kilometre flight of terrace. It is flanked by cafés embowered in tree-tops that overlook the ground beneath. Another ramp takes us to a second promenade two storeys above the first. On one side of it is a Rue de la Paix of the smartest shops; the other commands an uninterrupted view of the city's limits. Yet a third ramp leads to the esplanade along which the clubs and restaurants are grouped. We are sheer above the expanse of parks with a tossing sea of verdure plumb beneath us. And to the right and left, over there, and further away still, those gigantic and majestic prisms of purest transparency rear their heads one upon another in a dazzling spectacle of grandeur, serenity, and gladness . . .

'Those hanging gardens of Semiramis, the triple tiers of terraces, are "streets of quietude". Their delicate horizontal lines span the intervals between the huge vertical piles of glass, binding them together with an attenuated web . . . That stupendous colonnade which disappears into the horizon as a vanishing thread is an elevated one-way autostrada on which cars cross Paris at lightning speed . . . When night intervenes the

[28] First published *Architectural Review*, November 1957.

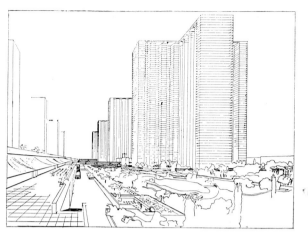

115. Fragment of paper table cloth from Paris restaurant

116. Le Corbusier's *ville radieuse*

passage of cars along the autostrada traces luminous tracks that are like the tails of meteors flashing across the summer heavens.'

This quotation is from a piece called *The Street* which originally appeared in *L'Intransigeant* in May, 1929. It is a description of the Plan Voisin, a project of 1925 which applied the principles and building types of Le Corbusier's earlier project Une Ville Contemporaine (1922) to Paris.

We still respond to this dream but we no longer believe in the means by which he imagined it could be achieved. His city is a colossal, axially organised, chess board.

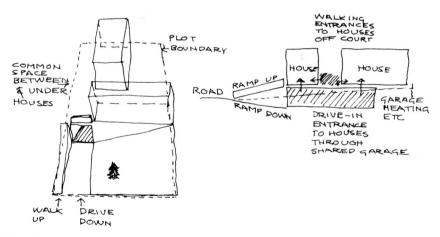

117. Sketches of le Corbusier's Maisons Jaoul. Changed relation of building, site and circulation in a viably motorised world

What we are after is something more complex, and less geometric. We are more concerned with 'flow' than with 'measure'. We have to create architecture and town planning which, through built form, can make meaningful the change, the growth, the flow, the vitality of the community.

There must be inherent in the organisation of every building the renewal of the whole community structure. Take, for example, the problem of rebuilding three houses in an existing street. The houses on each side of the street form with the street itself a distinct urban idea; the three new houses should not just live off this old idea, but should give an indication, a sign, of a new sort of community structure. But this cannot be done unless the architect has a more or less completely conceived general idea or ideal towards which all his work is aimed.

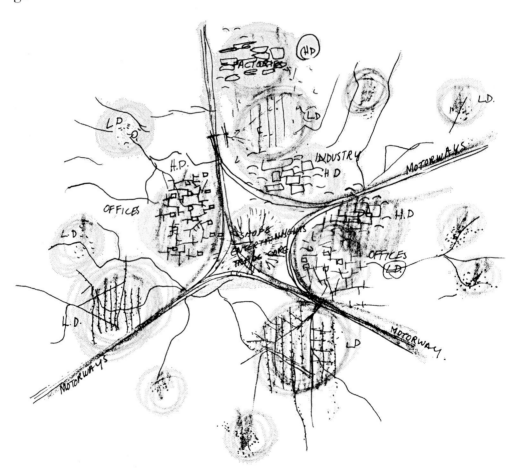

118. Cluster city. Population clusters: each working or living in types of buildings that have their own appropriate relation to motor traffic

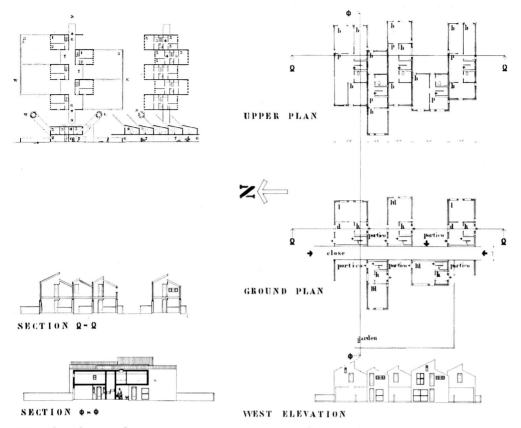

UPPER PLAN

GROUND PLAN

SECTION Ω-Ω

SECTION Φ-Φ

WEST ELEVATION

119. Close house plans, sections and elevations; giving an orderly and urban aspect, even to areas of fairly low density where the houses have large private gardens

The general idea which fulfils this requirement is the concept of the Cluster. The Cluster is a close knit, complicated, often moving aggregation, but an aggregation with a distinct structure. This is perhaps as close as one can get to a description of the new ideal in architecture and town planning.

Given this description the problem of building the three houses in an existing street is one of finding a way (while still responding to the street idea) to chop through the old building face and build up a cluster complex in depth – a suggestion, a sign, of the new community structure.

It is traditionally the architect's job to create the signs or images which represent the functions, aspirations and beliefs of the community, and to create them in such a way that they add up to a comprehensible whole. The Cluster concept provides us with a way of creating new images of the city, and of deploying more meaningfully solutions which have already been put forward to deal with the problems of traffic, for

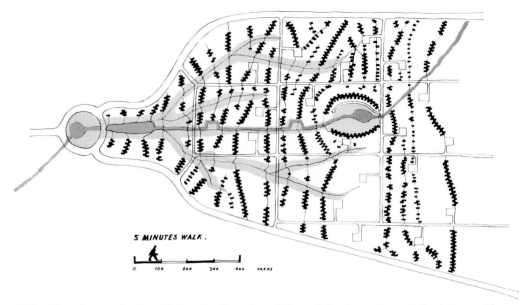

120. Close house cluster. Motor traffic enters this vertebrate system at the interruptions in the runs of buildings, and it parks there without penetrating further

example, motorways between cities, urban motorways, peripheral parking round the old centre, out of town shopping centres, off-motorway factories, and residential dormitories.

The accepted concept of the city is one of concentric rings, gradually decreasing to the edges in residential density and ground coverage, with a radial road pattern from the historic nodal point.

In the Cluster concept there is not one 'centre' but many. Areas of high intensity of use, related to industry, to commerce, to shopping, to entertainment, would be distributed throughout the community, and connected to each other and to frankly residential dormitories and dormitory-used villages by urban motorways. It is useless to pretend that

121. Close house system. For genuinely suburban development the houses are distributed along pedestrian ways that they enclose and partly cover

132

122. Close houses ride the landscape. Urban, yet without destroying the feel of the landscape

our lives are so simple that we can all 'live where we work'. We have to accept that families have more than one 'worker' in them and that choice of where one lives is a complex matter. Our job is to give choice; to make places that are meaningfully differentiated; to offer true alternative life-styles.

We must think out for each place the sort of structure which can grow, and yet be clear and easily understood at each stage of development. The word Cluster gives the spirit of such a structure, and existing planning techniques such as the control of residential densities and floor-space indices, comprehensive re-development and compulsory purchase, give the power (at least in England) to guide it. There seems no reason why more freely flowing, more varied, more useful communities cannot be constructed.

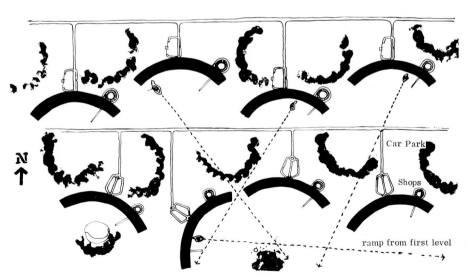

123. Terraced housing; development in depth. The slabs are orientated for view and light, and to give varying sense of (never total) enclosure

133

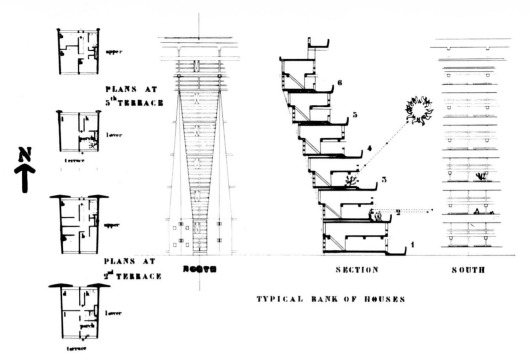

124. Elevation and plan of terraced housing. Parking is treated as one of the group of communal facilities at the base of each curved slab

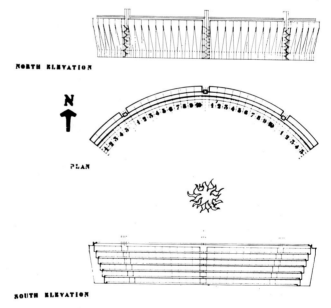

125. Detail of plan, elevations and section for terraced housing. Pedestrian circulation is by superimposed street decks, arranged to avoid dizzying vertical views. The building type has a sufficiently strong character to make its own visual order, even when distributed as high density infill to start to redefine a cluster pattern for a city

134

Besides the dialogue with Team 10 architects there was the actual experience of a truly motorised society.
*   The following letter is printed more or less fully because in it are the seeds of virtually all subsequent essays right up to the present time.*

13 Letter to America[29]

[29] Published *Architectural Design*, March 1958.

A first visit to America is a serious thing. Expecting to be asked to compare the state of architecture in America with that in Europe, a short formal statement was prepared before the visit:

"The architectural situation in the U.S.A., as far as one can judge from photographs and written material, is that there is still basically a belief in square, 'rational' architecture – a continuing to live of the impulses of 1913.[30]

Even when new structural forms (e.g. doubly curved shells) are introduced, or new materials (e.g. plastics), they are styled in the old International Style way.

The exception to this, at the unconscious level, seems to be the curtain wall building (as in Lever House), which while consciously 'square' architecture, actually transcends it: what is supposed to be academic Mies ends up as something else. The conscious exception is in the half comprehended, ideological writing and project work of Louis Kahn, where something approaching the European new way of thinking seems to be present.

And, of course, there is Charles Eames.

In general, from our side of the Atlantic it looks as if the American architect accepts the social and building-type status quo. He takes the given object and styles it 'Modern'.

The situation in Europe is that the 1913 impulses have become pretty weak, and they no longer seem spiritually valid, or their formal solutions applicable to architecture.

The rejection of the Modern Architecture canon means that we have had to examine the situation 'as found' and interpret this situation. This attitude is producing what we have called elsewhere an 'aesthetic of change'.

In younger architects the trend is ideologically well established; in fact, the ideological period of the New Modern Architecture is over and only awaits the opportunity to get on to the ground and into our lives.

You may ask, what are the characteristics of the New Modern Architecture in Europe? It is pragmatic (its basis is a sort of active socio-plastics) rather than old-style rational (i.e. diagrammatic with right angles).

As to its imagery, the magic having flown from the rectangle it is much freer in its use of form, more rough and ready, and less complete and classical.

Technologically it accepts industrially produced components as the

---

[30] The first 'constructions' were done by Tatlin in 1913, as a direct result of his encountering Picasso's reliefs. At this point Cubism became architecture.

natural order of the architect's vocabulary, not as something special or magical that will do his work for him.

Its key words are: *cluster, growth, change* and *mobility*. Around which stones you can roll your own snowballs."

126. Downtown New York, where the streets are mediaeval

127. The shadow of the Empire State Building crossing six blocks, early on a high summer afternoon

It is now necessary in retrospect to try to measure that preconception of America against the reality.

What is impossible to imagine is the absolute difference between the two cultures – different mental furniture, different attitudes, different values. Different not in degree but in kind. One is completely unprepared for the 'folk-art' aspect of American architecture.

Edith Sitwell found Hollywood 'completely unspoilt'. American architecture is similarly uncomplicated by doubt and uncorrupted by concept – *aluminium folk-art*.

Now folk-art is generally of two kinds: either fine-art images or disciplines are used without understanding and therefore transformed; or there arises a natural imagery which is sometimes so fully realised that it

137

128. Penn Center, Pittsburg, 1957. Who is
winning – buildings or cars?

129. Two curtain-wall buildings facing
one another – and bang!

becomes 'art'; i.e. no considerations of 'fine' or 'folk' are relevant. Most
American architecture is folk-art of the first category; old-style European
images and disciplines, such as trabeated space definition and symmetry,
are used without understanding and are therefore transformed into
folk-art.

This is not so obvious when the buildings are known only from
magazines, where the photographs isolate the building from its context
and where they are studied one at a time with long intervals between. But
when the buildings one has gone specially to see mostly turn out to be
bi-axially symmetrical, whatever the circumstances or programme, one
comes to regard them as the buildings of metal working peasants which
by purist standards are not architecture at all.[31]

For in nearly all these buildings the accepted discipline (symmetry) is
so kicked around and generally ignored as to convince one that the

[31] Of course there are buildings in the second
category in America which transcend their
formative processes and become 'art' – things like
diners, trailers, etc.

acceptance was blind.[32] One can only assume that the neo-classical aesthetic techniques used by Mies and talked about by Philip Johnson, being misunderstood, have achieved a status comparable to Nationalism, to which unquestioning and unswerving loyalty is due.[33]

Squareness and symmetry are obviously a deep American folk-need, for all successful American cars are rectangular on plan and on all four elevations, and are roughly bi-axially symmetrical (projections of the bonnet and boot are more or less equal). From the top of buildings car-lots and streets are a mosaic of coloured rectangles – the origin of 'Broadway Boogie Woogie' is, for sure, the view from the top of the Empire State looking down into the streets and parking lots below.[34]

The only car which dared to be non-square – the Studebaker[35] – is rumoured every year to be going out of production due to loss of sales. However, motor cars in general seem nearer to American design truth than buildings. In building there seems too easy an acceptance of outworn European modes, and an evasion of responsibility for creating genuine American organisational and aesthetic techniques.

The things a European most values from American culture are the throw-away objects, such as the magnificent magazines, advertising and packages. In the refrigerators and motor cars, as in heavy earth-moving equipment and freight trains, the feeling for American values is communicated through an imagery created without self-consciousness.

There is the same feeling in Pollock. But American architecture has not yet had its Pollock[36] and there is as yet no specifically American attitude to the specifically American evolving present. This is particularly obvious in town layout, for buildings are always self-contained islands whose disciplines and influences are considered to stop with their walls.

To the European the most telling landscape in the east is the New Jersey Flats, a back-yard world of refineries and factories and marshlands, criss-crossed with Skyways. This is the super-image of the American urban waste landscape – the urban excreta squeezed out from the old city over the last fifty years – and something like this is the industrial land-scape norm.[37]

And then there are those new suburbs.

[32] Throughout this letter the best buildings are being compared to the best elsewhere.
[33] See *The Organisation Man* on the Conformity Culture.
[34] After all Mondrian's talk about a constructed art he was forced back in the end to real imagery in order to renew himself.
[35] The 'square-look' was in fact invented by Raymond Loewy for Studebaker just after the war: previous to this American cars were beetles.
[36] 1966. It was probably Eames. But no-one in Europe told them so. Even the dates of their self-realisation accord.
[37] 1966. This is a landscape which seems to have always excited Europeans. There is a picture of it in Le Corbusier's *Urbanisme*, published in 1925.

The whole place is in a process of continual expansion and change which makes traditional architecture and town planning techniques simply not adequate.

Thinking about the problem of the permanent and the changing it would seem that some sort of 'fix', i.e. a system of permanent reference points, is necessary to the stability of the individual, and that a changing environment must take account of this need.

On the scale of the American environment such permanence would have to be pretty big. It might be possible to maintain a controlled, relatively unchanging background – say of agriculture or forestry, or, in the east, simply unused space – against which would be set a throw-away immediate environment. The 'background permanency', which would include the Freeways and be controlled by a super-authority, would be fairly stable; say major changes every twenty-five to fifty years. The throw-away environment of houses, supermarts, etc., would not be 'architecture' at all but things tossed out by industry in a number of models, like cars and washing machines (and which, incidentally, might keep the production economy afloat for a few more years). These houses, shops, crèches, etc., would be realised in a transient aesthetic, unlike the present housing environment, which is transient but which is realised through a permanent aesthetic.

Related to the 'background permanency' would be permanent-aesthetic buildings, the nodal or growth points to which the transient elements would be related. And even if one's prognostication of permanence proved wrong, at least some system would be under way in which both permanence and change would be given social and plastic value.[38]

Where car/refrigerator technology and standards are applied to building components the results are simply staggering. In fact, a wash-room on Madison can be a major architectural experience: a room about ten feet square, lined with mosaic, divided by a stove-enamelled partition and door with chrome fittings; a free-from-the-wall wc with a chrome pedal flush and no visible pipework; a free-from-the-wall wash-hand basin with beside it, flat with the mosaic, a floor-to-ceiling panel of unjointed and unframed stainless steel with slots for towel dispensing and disposal. It is impossible to communicate the feeling one has of a new sort of solidity, wealth and power in this quite unextraordinary American lavatory. And everything out of a catalogue.

The panels of the Alcoa building in Pittsburgh give the same feeling of industrial perfection. The glass curtain-wall is a typical example of what

[38] In discussion Paul Nelson pointed out the relevance of the MARS Plan for London to the problem of growth of cities.

140

technology, accepted without reservation, can do to otherwise indifferent buildings. For although the application of curtain-walls cannot be called a vernacular (as that implies a language), buildings which use them are undoubtedly better than they would have been if their architects had had to develop a brick and stone façade of their own. Glass and metal faced buildings give the maximum light reflection into the street and this in itself is a contribution to the city. And there are, moreover, magical distortions when two straight-up-and-down buildings are opposite one another. A blue glass city, no matter how organisationally banal, is never optically boring.

Seagram, of course, in dark brown glass and bronze, plays it so cool that everything else now looks like a jumped-up supermart.

Chicago[39]

The importance of Chicago is that it is one of the few nineteenth century cities left. Other nineteenth century cities such as Liverpool, at least in their downtown area, have been confused by twentieth century building, but Chicago around the Loop is pure nineteenth century and is a perfect example of a period in which architects believed in the validity of the city as an idea and built towards it.

This was done without any loss of individuality or identity of buildings (and their Companies) or streets. The language of the architecture, the grid plan and zoning regulations, and the discipline of the Byelaws were aspects of a single town-building system combining to create a city with the unity and impact of the old European 'Art Cities' such as Florence or Augsburg. It is a town-building pattern of regular rectangular canyon streets.

One usually thinks of Chicago in terms of the warehouse structure inside and out – as in the Sears Roebuck Store (the Leiter Building, William le Baron Jenney 1889) – but the Marshall Field Store with its gorgeous white columned interiors soaring up floor upon floor, and with a unity between what is sold, the manner in which it is sold, and the building, makes Sullivan's Carson Pirie Scott Store look like the work of a man

[39] Written 1959. Previously unpublished.

141

who thinks acquisition is fundamentally wicked and to be discouraged.

But in the main it is serious 'Chapel' architecture that was the strength and is now the weakness of Chicago, now that the ethic and mood of America have changed. One cannot see them putting up with these stern difficult buildings much longer, although they are still strong and useful. I for one cannot really blame them. Although the new Inland Steel Building (by S.O.M.), breaking the old rules of regularly modulated full street frontages, makes one feel very sad at the passing of a genuine sophisticated system of town-building without anything really being offered in its place.

The sternness of the Chicago School is carried into the twentieth century by Frank Lloyd Wright. His Robie House (1909) and more particularly his Unity Temple (1906) are very serious buildings. The latter, I think, presents an interesting art-historical problem. Immediately on entering via the back premises I said to myself 'Mackintosh's Library, Glasgow School of Art'. It is something to do with the rectangular strip aesthetic, the elongations and exaggerations, and more particularly the integrations of the conduits and light fittings into the general aesthetic, that is common to both men and cannot be all coincidence – even if the similarity is only due to a common source (but what source for the integrations of conduits/gas pipes?).[40]

And the Glasgow School of Art is better. If there is any direct influence there is no doubt of the direction it was travelling; although the Art School Library wing was not built until 1907–9, the main building with its marvellous staircase was designed in 1896, and the first section completed in 1899. And in 1896 Frank Lloyd Wright was still building in Oak Park houses almost indistinguishable from their neighbours, and certainly he had not yet hit his style (e.g. Nathan G. Moore House, Oak Park, 1895).

Always colours combined with the enormous eaves give the interiors the character of a mortician's parlour. They are gloomy – indeed spooky – in the extreme and it is this art nouveau quality which separates his work from that of the later international modern architecture (i.e. Le Corbusier and the Germans) which was essentially full of light.

Between the 1900s and the 1950s Frank Lloyd Wright's 'free plans' produce an intestinal play of spaces (especially obvious in the Knossian gloom of the Johnson Wax Building and in the Guggenheim Museum), whereas the spaces in the new architecture were at worst *normal* (regular, well-lit and hygienic) and at best *poetic* (somehow the light itself was modelled – light everywhere, no gloom – as in Le Corbusier's Maison

[40] Peter Blake says that the Japanese Temple in the Chicago Fair of 1893 is a key influence for F.L.W. – so Japan may be the common source.

142

la Roche and in the Villa Savoie). This joyousness of early modern architecture had only one precursor – the house of Charles Rennie Mackintosh.

And in a curious way Mies van der Rohe's work in Chicago has both these characteristics, normality *and* light-filled poetic space.

The form of the city must correspond to the pattern of human associations as we now see them. We see them as looser knit, in a social situation more open and changing than in the past. For the city to correspond to this view of society it must have better systems of physical communication and new form concepts through which society can recognise and realise its new self. And in fact, for architects, the two things are wrapped up with each other, for putting increased emphasis on mobility involves throwing over traditional aesthetic values which were mostly concerned with fixed relationships; and, on the other hand, Cartesian aesthetics have to be rejected, since they are incapable of carrying the cultural load of our time. All this inevitably leads to an 'aesthetic of change'.

14 Mobility[41]

Mobility has become the characteristic of our period. Social and physical mobility, the feeling of a certain sort of freedom, is one of the things that keeps our society together, and the symbol of this freedom is the individually owned motor car.

[41] First written 9th February 1958. First published *Architectural Design*, October 1958.

Mobility is the key to town planning, both socially and organisation-ally, for it is not only concerned with roads but with the whole concept of a mobile, fragmented community. That road-systems have a special role in the realisation of such a community is implicit in the 'Cluster City' idea, but they were not dealt with in detail before because it was felt to be more important to present the concept as an ideal, and as an aesthetic, first.

Roads, together with the main transit lines, power lines and drains, form the essential infra-structure of the community. The most important thing about roads is that they are physically big, and have the same power as any big topographical feature, such as a hill or a river, to create geographical, and in consequence social, divisions. To lay down a road therefore, especially through a built-up area, is a very serious matter for one is fundamentally changing the social structure.

Traditionally some unchanging large-scale thing – the Acropolis, the River, the Canal, or a unique configuration of the ground – was what made the whole community structure comprehensible, and assured the identity of the parts within the whole.

Today our most obvious failure is the lack of comprehensibility and identity in big cities, and the answer is surely in a clear, large-scale road system; the urban motorway lifted from an ameliorative function to a unifying one. In order to perform this unifying function all the roads must be part of a system. The backbone of the system must be the motorways in the built-up areas themselves, where their very size in relation to other development makes them capable of doing the visual and symbolic unifying job at the same time as they actually make the whole thing work.

To be physically positive the roads must run in a neutralised zone of green planting or constructed landscape, whichever does the job best. Such a neutralised zone can be seen in action along the old Merritt Parkway which runs through endless suburban housing areas. If one could see these houses the drive would be a nightmare, and if the Parkway did not exist the amorphousness on either side would have nothing to relate to.

Of course in the dense, built-up areas of big cities the problems of movement are more complicated than those on a Parkway out of town.

Inter-sector and local (low speed car/pedestrian) traffic should have separate systems which offer no short cuts. All movement must proceed through each stage of the hierarchy –

and the town-building should respond to this hierarchy of movement.

Louis Kahn's plan for Midtown Philadelphia[42] demonstrated how movement can be organically re-organised so that it is one with its inter-related functions of parking, shopping, etc.

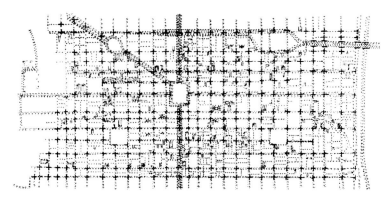

130. Louis Kahn's diagram of existing movement pattern, Philadelphia. In Kahn's words the diagram is 'to redefine the use of streets and separate one type of movement from another – through streets, go streets (free of trollies, buses and parked vehicles), stop streets for staccato movement, docks for deliveries and pedestrian ways'

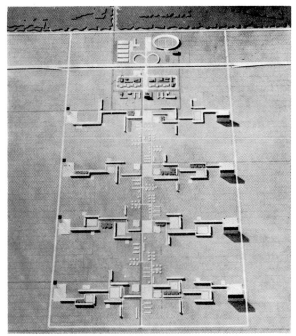

131. Alexander polder plan 1956, by Bakema and Opbouw

The idea of relating the architecture to the type of movement is most easily shown first of all in an example uncomplicated by existing conditions.

[42] See *Perspecta 2.*

146

The 1956 plan for Alexanderpolder (by J. B. Bakema and Opbouw) has a low-speed road at its centre, meandering backwards and forwards serving family houses on the ground; and the direct town-speed road runs around the periphery where the buildings are large Unités at quarter-mile intervals.

The problems in an existing town are more difficult. A typical situation occurs where a new urban motorway is driven through a built-up area following an old street, one side being torn down to accommodate it.

The side that is left consists of six-storey commercial buildings from the nineteenth century, with domestic-type windows and a doorway on to the street.

How are we to infill or re-develop on the existing side which now faces on to a six-lane highway?

It is somehow not right to rebuild to the old pattern, yet continuity of frontage may be the only merit the old development had, and this should not be lightly thrown away.

The noise has increased by ten times since horse and cart days, and there is no direct access from the new road.

Should the building therefore face the motorway at all? – would it not be more correct for the building to have its back to the motorway, and an indication on this back that one would find entry and the life of the building on the other side?

If one considers movement as the mainspring of urban building, radical forms come into being.

In the Hauptstadt Berlin Plan (Alison and Peter Smithson with Peter Sigmond, 1958) the separate systems for cars and pedestrians, each with its own discipline and aesthetic, allow the fullest possible human experience of the various sorts of movement.

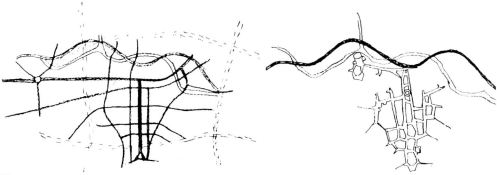

Hauptstadt Berlin 1958. Project by the authors and Peter Sigmond.
132. Street system   133. Pedestrian system

In small villages in Germany people gather on fine Sundays at vantage points overlooking the autobahn just to see the cars go by. And

134. Flyover near Montabaur. The Cologne-Limburg autobahn through Westewald

this is a very moving experience, for one feels in contact with the life-stream of Europe, and not just of Germany.

So, in this Berlin Plan we have: cars as spectacle ⇓ look down to roads: people as spectacle ⇑ look up to escalators and terraces.

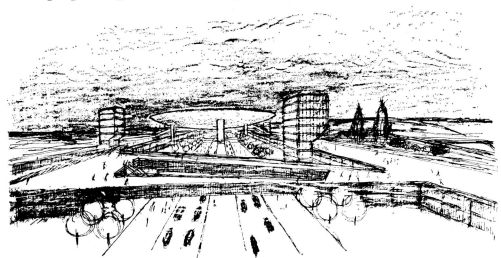

135. Movement systems

To enhance the particular form of movement streets are straight and direct. And the pedestrian platform is free and irregular, providing routes and spaces for the random patterns of pedestrian movement, and the eye is directed down to the streets below.

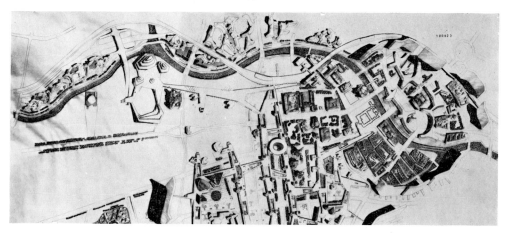

136. Hauptstadt Berlin 1958. In the centre is the upper level network of pedestrian communication linking the shopping, entertainment and office areas. (Axonometric drawing by Peter Sigmond)

Systems of access are also places.

Consider for example the social implications of the arrangement of houses around a small parking lot, or turn-around, which puts all movement under continuous social scrutiny.

The opportunity for opting-out of a given social situation seems to be one of the reasons why people have chosen to build and to live in cities, even if their 'neighbourhood' is in Surrey or New England. To be free in one's associations, and not forced by the size or structure of the community into unchosen relationships from which it is impossible to escape, is a genuine twentieth-century necessity.

Car movement is flow movement; not the irregular stopping and starting, changing direction, turning around, of the walker.

To flow means to move evenly at speeds to suit functions, from fast on national roads, to slow on house access roads.

137. Los Angeles. Freeway intersection at night. Cars as spectacle of lights in movement

138. Port Authority bus terminal, New York. Movement building

In new layouts the road/building relationship should indicate the relative importance of the route. In an existing road system this could be done with coloured markers,[43] and at night by coloured light.

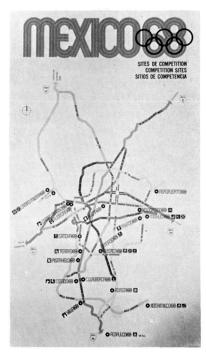

139 Mexico City 1968 Olympic map showing colours allocated to the routes to various event locations. The roads, street furniture, trees were actually banded in colour

[43] This was done to Mexico City for the Olympic Games 1968, simply with coloured paint.

140. Buenos Aires at night. Movement in lights in the city

In conclusion: to fly, ride a horse, sail a boat, are all distinct sensations. We must have this directness and sensation of freedom for the car.

The first step is to realise a system of urban motorways. Not just because we need more roads, but because only they can make our cities an extension of ourselves as we now wish to be.

141. Tokyo Expressway No. 4, near Kandabashi. Built movement

142. Garage; advertisement tear-sheet. Our cities – an extension of ourselves as we now wish to be?

The object of the next essay was to define the aesthetics of change; the form systems that follow naturally from the ideas of Mobility, Cluster, and so on.

15 Aesthetics of change[44]

The necessity, the inevitability, of a new sort of architecture arises out of our new situation, and can best be demonstrated by taking a simple example, one in which the shortcomings of present methods of building are most obvious.

143. The neo-classical tradition. Königsplatz, Munich, by Von Klenze

[44] First published in *Architects' Year Book 8*, 1957.

The older universities are textbook examples to show that a human organisation can realise itself in built-form as a 'thing'. That is, they are comprehensible as a whole, more than the sum of their parts, built up through a clear language of form, and potentially capable of endless renewal. The fact that the universities have survived from the Middle Ages into the twentieth century is proof that their social organisation is continually being renewed to meet new cultural objectives. But in this century they have failed to renew themselves physically. They are living off built capital, off what the Middle Ages and the Renaissance have left them.

The original colleges were closed communities of individual rooms with a common hall and chapel. The relationship between the individual and the collective was expressed by a complex of in-looking courts, with one point of contact between the rest of the world and the college. At their founding they were really closed, all teaching was done in college and they were outside the jurisdiction of the town of which they formed part.

In modern times more and more teaching is done by the 'University' – by the various 'faculties', and the relationship with the town has become more open.

The built structure reflects this change. During the seventeenth, eighteenth and nineteenth centuries, museums, libraries and faculty buildings, taking the form of great solid blocks of building, have been

144. The neo-classical tradition. Project by Schinkel

worked into the interstices between the colleges. The new pattern was one of enclosed college buildings, and open-to-all, compact faculty buildings.

Unfortunately we are now faced with an entirely new situation. The acquisition of knowledge since the technological revolution requires new techniques, mechanised experimental techniques, which have to be housed in vast buildings of a completely new sort. These new techniques are not confined to the newer disciplines, such as physics, chemistry, engineering, etc., but have also revolutionised medicine, mathematics, and the humanities.

The physical change of the university pattern necessary to meet the needs of these new techniques presents architects with a problem of an entirely new order, in which the relationship between the colleges and the faculty buildings is changing, and where the physical growth of the whole town and university demands a completely different order of scale in the parts.

A realistic approach would be to consider, first of all, the new 'flow' pattern. The colleges are no longer sufficient unto themselves, but debouch students into the old town circulation system to find their way to the faculty buildings. Any new building must establish a 'flow' relationship to the whole pattern of movement of the university and town. And this 'flow' relationship must be reflected in the aesthetic of the new building – the form it takes.

Secondly, we must consider the question of change of scale. In classical aesthetic theory the part and the whole were in a finite relationship one with the other, the aesthetic of each being 'closed'. The part indicates by its actual size and its scale the size of the whole. But as we have seen, the university and town are changing and growing. So new buildings should show by their 'scale in change' the 'size in change' of the whole complex; yet still indicate limits. And their aesthetic should be an 'aesthetic of change', postulating a relationship with something that does not yet exist. Their shape must not only be able to 'take' change, but should imply change.

The project we made in 1953 for the University of Sheffield shows the new aesthetic technique in action. The problem was to add an enormous volume of new faculty buildings on to an existing 'red brick' university. The site available was small and cut into two parts by a main road. A conventional solution of separate lumps for each faculty would leave little space on the ground, and that space would be cut about by student and service circulation.

The alternative was to create a continuous 'flow' complex, tracking the periphery of the site, with a street-in-the-air at its middle level. In addition to the street-deck, the existing and the new buildings are linked by a high-level 'bridge' which finally crosses the main road to the student recreation buildings. The scale of the whole layout is geared to the size of the new university, and the growing city of Sheffield. The general organisation of the 'separate' parts of the complex implies their ultimate linkage, and their detailed aesthetic is one of change. The rooms can be re-arranged in height and length to meet changing faculty requirements, the façades being built up from screens (linked to the internal screen system) which change without fuss to reflect any change within.

To find a built example of the new aesthetic we have to look at the Eames's House at Santa Monica, California. Built in 1949 its apparent casualness implies 'change', a message carried both by its aesthetic, and by its genuine lightness.

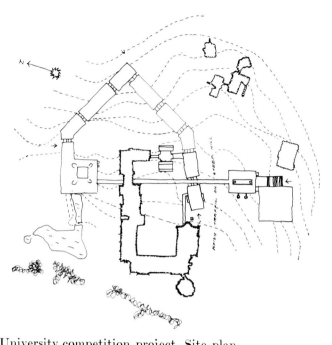

145. Sheffield University competition project. Site plan

146. Sheffield University. Library façade seen from the park, the route entering from the right

This building's aesthetic of expendability is quite outside the European tradition, but if we need transient buildings we must face up to creating a transient aesthetic.

147. The Eames's house, Santa Monica, California. (cf illustration 171)

The 'Cluster City' idea involves a redistribution of densities, a spreading about of the 'points of intensity'.
  The following essay continues to explore this theme.

16 Scatter[45]

There are two fundamental questions we have to find answers for; first, what is the optimum density for various sorts of family life; and second, is there still a need for a paramount 'city centre', a place of community identification?

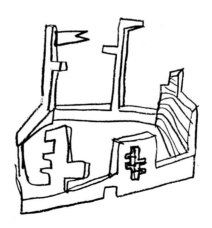

148. Scatter ideogram

[45] First published by *Architectural Design*, April 1959.

Now the first question is tied up with the increased availability of personal transport, and the relationship of the car to the house. If the car is to be a convenience and a pleasure it must be easy to use. A family excursion with babies and baskets and buckets and spades, from the fifteenth floor of an access balcony two-lift slab block, via a distant underground garage, can be no picnic, and we can assume that more and more people will want to take their pleasure in such excursions.

Then there is the problem of the real space-needs of family life, especially for children. Everyone needs a bit of sheltered outdoor space as an extension to his house. This space can also serve the needs of children up to two or three years old, but from then on children need more and more space. Space to play safely close by until seven years old or so, and space for wild running and little excursions until eleven, and then places to go and do things in until they are almost grown up.

None of these requirements can be met simply and pleasurably at densities much above 70 p.p.a.[46]

Unfortunately, almost all known sorts of low-density development are inadequate, in their form, in their system of construction, and in their system of access. And, most serious of all, they are 'culturally obsolete'. For it is not only a question of finding the right living pattern for our present way of life, and the equipment that serves it, but also a question of finding the correct symbols to satisfy our present cultural aspirations.

In the past few years we have made various projects which attempt to face up to these needs.

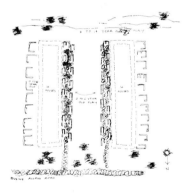

149. Strip Appliance House. Group plan

150. Strip Appliance House. The portico rows screened by garages in 'no fines' painted white

[46] 1966. We now believe that these requirements can be achieved with densities of between 100 and 150 p.p.a.

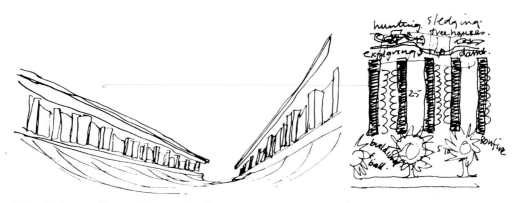

151. Strip Appliance House. (*Left*) Anonymous communal space, open-ended to communal activity areas (sledging, bonfires etc). (*Right*) Pedestrian access only in covered way. Parking in layby in garage area off service road at ends of rows

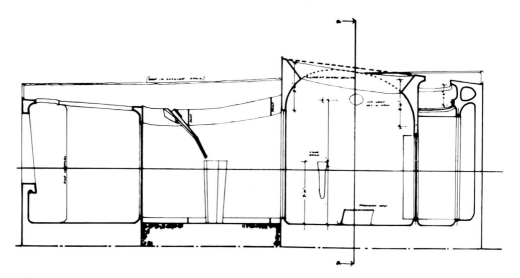

152. House of the Future. Section

The density of the Appliance Houses (Strip Appliance House, Snowball Appliance House, 1958) is about 30 p.p.a. A single storey carpet of 'House of the Future' patio houses, with adequate green gaps for play spaces, gives a density of round about 60 p.p.a. And the arrangement of apartment houses on tiered terraces in parkland would be practical at about 70 p.p.a.

Of course there are lots of people to whom 'hotel life', by which is meant the maximum of privacy, anonymity and simplicity of service, is suitable and pleasurable. Perhaps for 40 per cent of the population of big

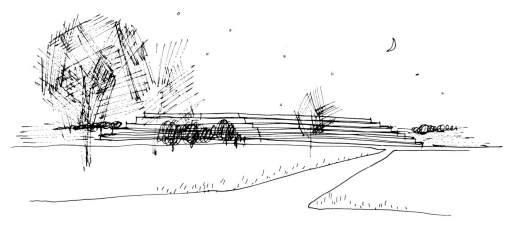

153. Terraced housing. Perspective in landscape

cities, especially where the population is growing older. These people are in fact well served by conventional forms of high building for which Mies van der Rohe's Lake Shore Drive apartments are the model, or Swedish point blocks, where the access is swift, secret and completely enclosed, and the windows look out into anonymous space. Such buildings situated near the city centres give a maximum of convenience for students, single people, childless couples, and grown-up families. Their density can be very high indeed, up to 300 p.p.a.

Much of our post-war housing effort has gone into providing high-flat buildings very suitable for hotel-type living, but unfortunately they have been provided for the use of families with children. To go on doing this would be ridiculous.

Family living, except in exceptional circumstances, is best served by relatively low density development, wherever its location.

For a human agglomeration to be 'a community' in the twentieth century it is not necessary, practically or symbolically, for it to be a dense mass of buildings, but that does not necessarily mean that for the same population a bigger overall area need be covered than at present. It is essentially a matter of re-grouping densities. There is no need, for example, for low-density family houses to be excluded from the central areas of the city, nor is there any need to think conventionally that housing nearer the country must be at low densities. The overall pattern of the community could be one of clusters of varying densities, with many parts, as high as 300 p.p.a. Such concentrations will allow for the creation

163

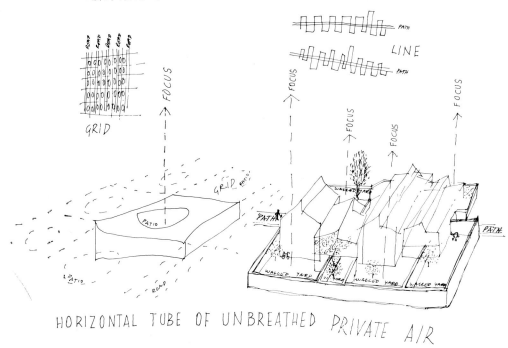

VERTICAL TUBE OF UNBREATHED PRIVATE AIR

GRID

LINE

FOCUS

HORIZONTAL TUBE OF UNBREATHED PRIVATE AIR

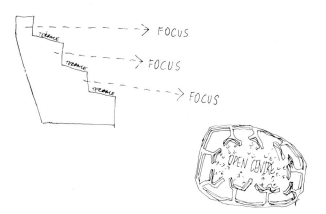

FOCUS

FOCUS

FOCUS

OPEN CENTRE

154. Private air diagrams: House of the Future; terraced housing, etc

of the new road/green space system and would compensate for centrally located low density development.

The second question left unanswered in the general exposition of the Cluster City idea was whether there is still a place for a 'city centre'. The implication was that there was no one centre. At the residual historic core one supposes there would survive those parts of government, big business, administration, etc., which are dependent on direct contact of person to person. They need a common meeting ground – restaurants, clubs, theatres, parks, shops, and so on. This is one reason for a centre.

Another is that although mass production has already made most goods widely available locally, and in the future this may well remove the need to 'go to town' to buy things, shopping is one of the few group activities we freely involve ourselves in. Going to town to shop is essentially a social gesture, an act of communion, of identifying oneself with a group.

The mystical, absolute centre will probably move about, migrate from place to place as our need for identification changes its focus. But an extraordinary myth-establishing built-place might still cause it to settle.

Primitive man is incapable of physical survival without group action; and modern man is incapable of mental survival without group thought / behaviour / things which persuade him that he is real. Form and myth keep him going.

17 The function of architecture in cultures-in-change[47]

Architecture is concerned with finding the pattern of buildings and communications which makes the community function and, at the same time, gives it meaning. To make the community comprehensible to itself – to give it identity – is also the work of the politician and the poet, but it is the work of the architect to make it visible. The way he did this in the past was to create building types which by themselves read 'house' or 'church' or 'shop', and which in combination read 'particular community'.

The type-images for the various functions within the culture give general legibility, and the variations and systems of combination give the exact identity to a particular group. The Romans, for example, found the forms that corresponded to their myth of themselves in the portico for the civil building, the colonnade for the public place or street, the atrium for the house, and in the straight road. These forms carried the concept of Rome across the world; from Baalbec to St Albans the same forms were used. Dealing with local conditions and climate was to them secondary to establishing their general idea of order. (But the local conditions were nevertheless efficiently dealt with.)

[47] First published *Architectural Design*, April 1960.

An ordering on this scale is built up through time, piece by piece, myth serving myth, image supporting image, until it appears that the whole is inevitable and unalterable. And then suddenly the whole thing ceases to satisfy, and disintegrates from lack of conviction.

At the present time, form-giving impulses emanate on the whole from Europe, the United States, South America, and Japan. An excellent example of the working of these impulses can be seen in the state capital for the Punjab at Chandigarh, by Le Corbusier. At Chandigarh an essentially Western ordering was enlarged to meet local environmental and human requirements, but in the buildings you can still read 'Mediterranean Basin 1950'. And it is not easy to see what else is possible, for only a person embedded in a culture can exactly define and re-project its potential, and when this potential is low it is surely better to import a live plant that may seed, than to plant dead trees.

The responsibility of architects working in countries of great social change for directing the culture potential is very great, and it is mostly being evaded.

155. The function of architecture in cultures-in-change. The court in the Palace of Diocletian at Split (Spalatto). The order of Roman architecture is the same right across the Roman world

167

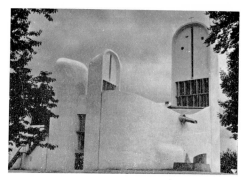

156. Model of the Governor's Palace at Chandigarh. Le Corbusier's Chandigarh is essentially 'European', although its location demanded a special effort from him

157. Chapel at Ronchamp. Le Corbusier used memories of older peasant societies as other people use bricks

In Casablanca in the fifties the accepted solution for mass housing (which was very good by, say, South African standards) was to replace the Bidonvilles (shanty towns) with courtyard houses, laid out on a regular grid which gave approximately the standards of accommodation and convenience of the houses in the villages beyond the Atlas where the people had come from.

158. Medenine, Tunisia. A postcard widely known in Purist circles in the 'twenties

159 Medenine, 1968

But these people now worked in a big city, and within weeks of their first arrival their aspirations would be towards better standards of living than they were used to in their villages, and their values would have been modified. And such changes of social objectives are likely to be much more violent as the media of mass communication extend themselves.

160. Maison Jaoul, Paris; le Corbusier. Peasant carcass and factory infill. A master-work on the knife edge of peasantism

169

161. Santorin. Aegean islands were also part of le Corbusier's mental baggage

In this circumstance, to give these new city dwellers, perhaps working in factories or in hotels, a more hygienic version of the mediaeval village house, can only be a stop-gap solution. And it is perhaps no solution at all, culturally speaking. What is good about the Atbat buildings is that they manage to be North African, and yet they are not simply an academic re-statement of traditional North African forms, and they do not try to ignore the existence of the dynamic technology and aesthetic of European architecture of the immediate past, especially Le Corbusier's in the 1920's. Yet they do not copy that, either. A genuine new image has been created, but it exists in isolation and the architects are being given no further opportunities to extend the pattern. It may be that these architects, one Russian, one Greek and one American (although all domiciled in France), because they are so culturally diverse, were able to put their finger on what was necessary in this particular culture at that moment.

But . . . in situations where there are acute changes in the way of life, the patterns of the community cannot be based on traditional or tribal

170

162. Housing at Casablanca; Atbat. One of the seminal buildings of the post-war architectural movement

163. A village beyond the Atlas mountains

164. Project for housing at Casablanca. One of the amazing Atbat models brought by Candilis and Woods to the CIAM congress at Aix en Provence. The little sun was bright yellow

usages or on religious laws, which are the crystallisation of former necessities for survival into poetic and formal patterns. In such situations the only thing that architects can do is to constitute themselves as image-making ginger-groups who try to face up to the problems of the present.

165. Pessac, near Bordeaux

166. Pessac, near Bordeaux, 1925. (Photographed 1957). The first built housing group of le Corbusier. The Atbat aesthetic remembers and regains the vitality and promise of the heroic period

They must try to find out, for example, how to group houses together so that the group has identity and meaning within the community, and try to discover what form of community buildings can define the political and social objectives best. If entertainment, instruction and commerce take place under a single roof could the community experience pride of collective ownership: what would be the real problems of control, of maintenance, of tenure?

The imagery and techniques which tropical countries are most likely to draw on are those of Brazil or Mexico or Venezuela, because they have vitality and glamour and are realised through relatively simple technologies. But these buildings arise out of a Baroque culture, which still conceives of buildings as isolated monuments, each sufficient unto itself, and they are still the products of rich old-style capitalist communities.

And it is no good looking to the climate and the physical environment to give the form of the building. A glass box and a mass-concrete cave can produce the same comfort conditions if one can afford the right mechanical equipment.

167. Temptation. The President's Palace, Brasilia

168. Philip Johnson House, New Canaan, Connecticut. Given the right equipment, and money, a concrete cave or glass box can be made to perform equally well in any conditions

169. Hostel at Ronchamp

It all depends what you are after. The shape of the culture can only be built up on separate, individual, form-giving decisions towards a common ideal, however vague this ideal may seem at present.

It is surely not right for a poor, socially-minded country to consider every building as a self-contained monument.

The consideration of the problems of the countries that are in obvious change – in Africa and the East – makes one realise how much our own culture is in change and needs a new image of itself. About this time, therefore, we started consciously to retrain ourselves.

'Due to the size and nature of modern communities, to bring about a real change, some areas of redevelopment need to be big in scale; large sections of a town, not buildings co-ordinated by planners. And this needs a special sort of engaged architecture. This is why we, and others, have for some time been agitating for the opportunity to develop an area in which the grouping characteristics can be carried from building to building into a freely organised whole; where the general objective is an active built-place, and not the creation of individual monuments in nineteenth century style, as in the Hansaviertel district of Berlin.'[48]

An edited version of the related pieces that follow was first published under the title 'Fix'. The original joint title was 'Cluster City 2'. These take up again the theme of 'Fix', for just as our mental processes need fixed points (fixed in the sense of change over a relatively long period) to enable them to classify and value transient information, and thus remain sane and lucid, so too, the city needs 'fixes' – identifying points with a long cycle of change, by means of which things changing on a shorter cycle can be valued and identified.

Chicago bus sign – One out of every 10 people is mentally sick.

[48] First published in *Architectural Review*, December 1960.

18 Fix: permanence and transience[49]

With a few things fixed and clear, the transient elements of the city no longer menace the sense of urban structure or the citizen's sanity, but can uninhibitedly reflect short-term needs and moods. If this distinction between the changing and the fixed were observed there would be less need for elaborate planning control over the appearance of every building, and legislative energy could be concentrated on long-term structure.

Historical buildings are often regarded as fixed in perpetuity; others, like law courts and municipal buildings, have almost unchanging functions, or, like power stations and heavy industrial plant, represent investments too massive to be altered frequently. These are the traditional architectural fixes. The architectural transients are the small buildings, particularly shops and houses, that are added to, altered or completely rebuilt on a short-term cycle of change.

The non-architectural environment is increasingly transient. Posters change every month, illuminated signs change every six months, and shop windows, clothing magazines and so on, arrive and disappear with great rapidity, in cycles related obscurely to each other.

Buildings should show the part they play in these cycles of change. 'Fixes' should look fixed and 'transients' transient, even if their actual life as buildings (so-called permanent constructions) is the same. To give an

[49] *Architectural Review,* December 1960

170. Crown Hall 1955, by Mies van der Rohe. With its formal plan, Crown Hall makes claims on eternity

example: Mies van der Rohe's Crown Hall at I.I.T. is a fix, and looks it, while Charles Eames' own house is a transient, and looks it. Both are built of steel and glass, and have roughly the same standard of permanence.

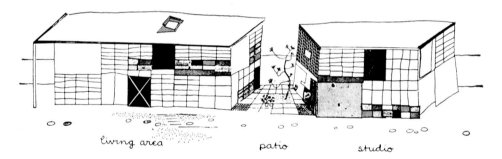

living area   patio   studio

171. The Eames's house. Double axonometric drawing. Transience and permanence are in the conception of a building, as much as in its material structure. Charles and Ray Eames's house, although built of steel, is conceived as a transient, almost casual structure

The one thing we are likely to get to which transient activity can be related is a special sort of road system, designed to act as a structure for the whole community. Neutralised by a green strip or built landscape, it need not be very large in relation to the town. Two or three great highways are almost sufficient to serve even Los Angeles, where motorisation is gradually approaching its saturation point of one car to every two persons.

172. Tokyo's motor-war. Akasaka-Mitsuke and its vicinity. What the fix looks like. How it can restore where amenity has been lost

Motorway patterns of this size may already be approaching the stable condition of the railway systems. And like them, will then probably go into a slow decline.

Such a road system is a 'fix' for movement running throughout the whole community, but the big motorway intersections, like the Los Angeles 'Mixmaster', or the San Francisco Skyway take-off for Oakland Bay Bridge, are more like traditional architectural fixes, and could properly be associated with existing architectural fixes where motorways serve, and ring, an historical centre. A whole network of motorways related to existing fixes in this way could serve not only for the purpose of travel, but also to define the areas into which the urban region is divided. In this way, also, the road system would help to keep our apparent level of mechanisation under control, for we can channel noise and excitement where they are needed, and create pools of calm where they are not.

An 'aesthetic of change', paradoxically, generates a feeling of security and stability by supplementing our ability to recognise the pattern of related cycles. Already we can recognise also that an adequate urban motorway system is a psychological as well as a functional requirement of an urban region: it offers the possibility of escape.

179

*An open society needs an open city. Freedom to move
and somewhere to go, both inside and outside the city.*

*It is this latter aspect which is most worth discussing
in detail, for it is in the question of social foci that the
difference between the Cluster City idea, and what it is
commonly compared with, Los Angeles, can be seen.*

19 Social foci and social space[50]

[50] First published in *Architectural Design*, December
1960.

173. Advertisements exploiting the desire for relaxation: *a*, the mountain cabin; *b*, Seine type; *c*, the open air; *d*, the woods

Los Angeles is fine in many respects, but it lacks legibility – that factor which ultimately involves identity, and the whole business of the city as a comprehensible extension of oneself. The layout of Los Angeles and the form of its buildings do not indicate places to stop and do things in. What form it has is in its movement pattern, which is virtually an end in itself.

It is quite clear that in an ideal city at the present time the communication net should serve (and indicate) places-to-stop-and-do-things-in. This is somewhat different from saying that every city needs a core. When Los Angeles is criticised for not being a city in the old European sense, it is not generally realised what a colossal scatter of places people go to do things in: to the mountains for a picnic; to the desert for a trip; to a far-off beach for a bathing party; or to Marshall Fields in Chicago for shopping. The social foci are almost all outside the so-called downtown, and they mostly have nothing in the way of buildings which could conventionally be 'moulded' to help the legibility of the town pattern.

But nevertheless there should be more to this business of community facilities than the convenience they offer to the citizen, and their counteraction to the wasteful exodus from the big cities which takes place every weekend. Community facilities are the raw material for the building of tangible stopping-places, for places where things can happen. Can be seen to be about to happen. Can cause things to happen?

174. Asian festivals and rallies; above, and next page

182

183

The only things we have got in the normal housing areas to build these places from – for houses cannot be made to speak of other things – are the high schools, the shops, and so on. Obviously the first stopping place beyond the housing groups should be built from these elements. There are no others we can use.

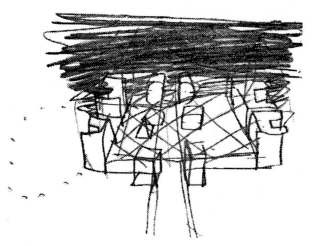

175. General view of the centre, with raised plaza and access towers

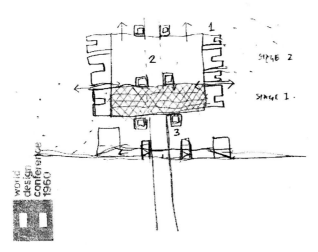

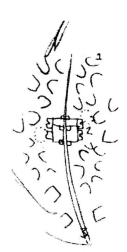

176. Location plan. Key: 1, housing groups 2, centre

177. Social space needs. Diagram showing the relation between housing, shops and schools. Key: 1, shops, nursery schools, primary schools etc. 2, plaza with parking underneath. 3, access towers, advertisements etc

184

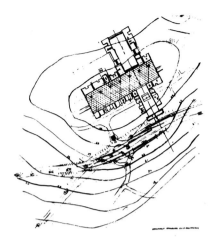

178. Steilshoop, Hamburg. Original setting-out sketch of the relation of centre to town-link road

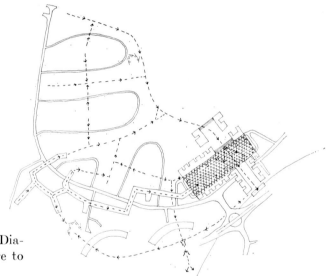

179. Steilshoop, Hamburg. Diagram of connection of centre to all movement routes

The community facilities should not be dumped down like items of an industrial plant in a void of green space where their impact is zero, and they are really only half 'working', but they should be so organised as to create social space.

This means not just putting a building on a site, but with a building making a place.

185

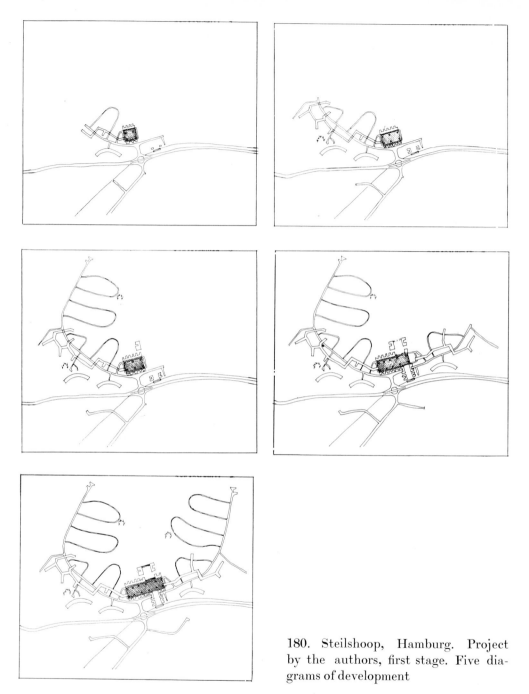

180. Steilshoop, Hamburg. Project by the authors, first stage. Five diagrams of development

Instead of the Chapel on its plot, the rates office on its plot, the school in its playing fields and gardens, can we not somehow make somewhere that can work at a far more general level, with real economy and meaning?

186

Appendix

ROBIN HOOD LANE

A housing scheme for the Greater London Council

Three small sites in the area of Robin Hood Lane, Tower Hamlets, became available for redevelopment by the then London County Council in 1963. For these sites (known as 'Manisty Street') we prepared designs for two separate buildings on a common theme, with access to the dwellings off 'decks'; which decks we hoped would ultimately be joined up with those of further buildings to be built when sites became available to form one big linked dwelling group.

181. Manisty Street Collage

Later, the Greater London Council (as the L.C.C. had now become) decided to speed up the clearance and demolition of a large group of obsolescent tenements – Grosvenor Buildings – on one of the adjacent sites. The original brief was withdrawn and a new, far more consolidated, site and a new programme brief to Parker Morris standards were given back to us for consideration in the spring of 1966.

In the interval a clearer picture of the future road network around the site had emerged, which together with the enlargement of the site area has led to a quite new variant of deck-accessed housing.

188

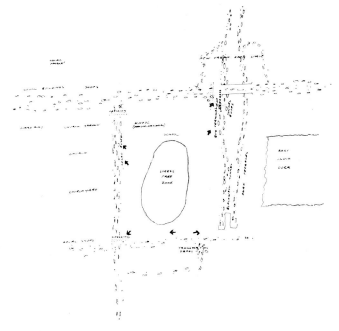

182. Robin Hood Lane. Traffic pattern. Desire routes of tenants

On the east of this enlarged site is the east side of the London Motorway Box, running in a cutting as it emerges from crossing under the Thames in the old and new Blackwall Tunnels.

On the west side of the site is Cotton Street – the main surface feeder-road to the Isle of Dogs, and to the north the East India Dock Road, now six lanes wide.

The housing site at Robin Hood Lane is thus traffic-exposed on three sides. We have therefore organised the site so as to create a 'stress-free' central zone protected from the noise and pressures of the surrounding roads by the buildings themselves. In this stress-free zone there is no vehicular movement whatever and there is therefore a quiet, green, heart which all dwellings share and can look out into.

On the fourth side, the old Poplar High Street is relatively free of traffic movement, and building development to the south is low. The lay-out has been kept open to this side, and it is thus possible to get long views out and the sun in.

For this sheltering, wall-like arrangement of the buildings a special dwelling-type has been developed in which the access decks and the living rooms are on the 'outside' nearest the noise, and the bedrooms and

189

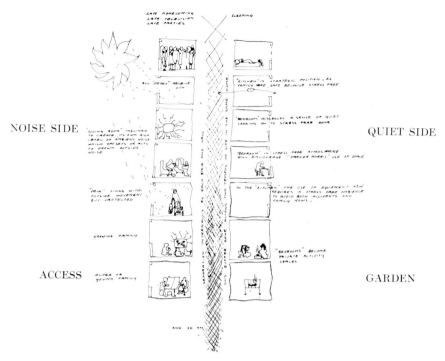

NOISE SIDE

QUIET SIDE

ACCESS

GARDEN

183. Robin Hood Lane. Reasoning behind the disposition of accommodation

dining-kitchens on the 'inside', away from the noise. To put the access decks and the living-rooms on the noisy side seemed to us correct insofar as the deck is bound to be fairly noisy and the living-room, being the chief common active area of the dwelling, will create its own level of ambient noise which 'acts' to drown outside noise.

However, the G.L.C. Housing Committee insisted quite reasonably that the sound level in the living-rooms with windows partly open should be below that recommended in the Wilson Report, which gives permissible noise levels in the living-rooms and bedrooms of dwellings in busy urban areas as:– Day: 50 dBA. Night: 35 dBA. The G.L.C.'s Scientific Officer carried out a noise survey on the roads around the site. From these measurements the worst '10% noise level' anywhere on the face of the proposed new buildings (assuming no protection other than distance between buildings and road) was, simply expressed:

	70–75 dBA during the day
Wilson Committee level required inside:	50 dBA
Therefore reduction needed:	20–25 dBA

190

'Partly open window' gives reduction:	10–15 dBA
Therefore further required reduction:	10 dBA
Assume reduction from planting but not walls:	5dBA
Further required reduction:	5 dBA approx.

To get better than this 5 dBA reduction we developed in collaboration with the G.L.C. Scientific Officer:

1. An acoustic absorbent lining at the window head;
2. A projecting sill to deflect direct sound from entering the horizontal centre pivot windows in their checked open position;
3. A system of projecting mullions to protect the side of the same windows, and to prevent sound travelling across the façades and from dwelling to dwelling;
4. A 10 foot high 'acoustic wall', canted over at the top to reflect noise back into the traffic, which runs immediately behind the pavement on the west (Cotton Street) side and as close as possible to the edge of the sunken approach to the Blackwall Tunnel on the east side.

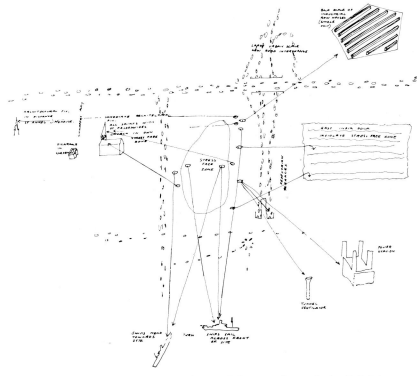

184. Robin Hood Lane. Visual connections of the people to their district

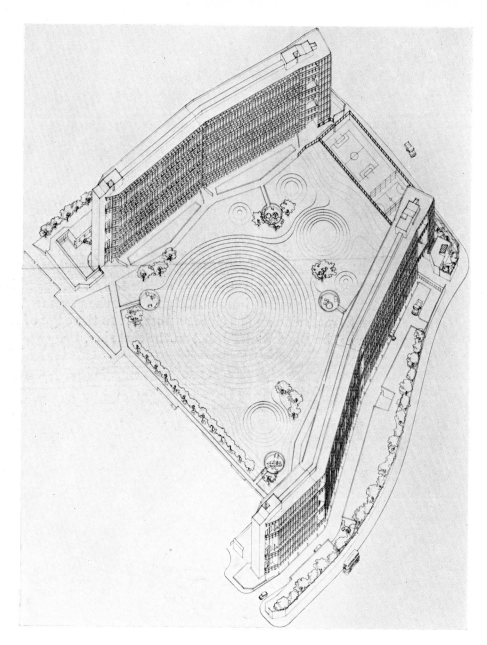

185. Robin Hood Lane. Axonometric drawing of general layout, stage 1. Large central green space protected by the buildings, the buildings themselves protected by an 'acoustic wall' at the pavement's edge with trees behind, and specially designed windows and mullions. Servicing and parking take place in a 'moat' between the buildings and the roads

On this particular site the living-rooms on the 'outside' get wonderful large-scale views of the docks, the river, and the famous East London churches.

The site was zoned by the G.L.C. planners for mainly residential use at a density of 136 persons to the acre. There is an 'open-space deficiency' in the area, and the large definable open space of the lay-out is part of the planning requirement to provide two-thirds of an acre per thousand persons out of residential land.

An existing market and shopping area at Lansbury (built as part of the 1951 'Festival of Britain' exhibition) is to be found about two hundred yards westward along the East India Dock Road, and a parade of eleven shops in the Poplar High Street within a few yards of the southern boundary of the site. To these existing facilities and to the local bus connections the main flows of people from the site are directed.

For the first stage of the development shown here, the calculated gross area for housing was 4·922 acres, which at a density of 141·8 p.p.a.[51] gives a site population of 698 persons, housed in the following way:

DWELLINGS

	Old People	2 person	3 person	4 person	5 person	6 person
NUMBER	38	26	26	60	54	10
%	18	12	12	28	25	5

All the Old People's dwellings are on the ground floor, as is their club-room.

About 70% of the dwellings have garages in the scheme as shown on the drawings, the remainder up to 100% will be added as demand builds up, by completing the part shown in the drawings in its temporary use as a hard-play area. There is also parking for visitors and guests.

All parking, servicing, storage, etc., takes place in a 'moat' below garden level, but still in the open air and therefore naturally ventilated and lit – using an idea first developed for the Mehringplatz project in 1962.

---

[51] The second stage which is nearest to the noisiest intersection – that of the East India Dock Road and the Motorway emerging from the Blackwall Tunnel – will, logically, be developed at a slightly lower density, to bring the overall density to the planning norm – least people nearest most noise.

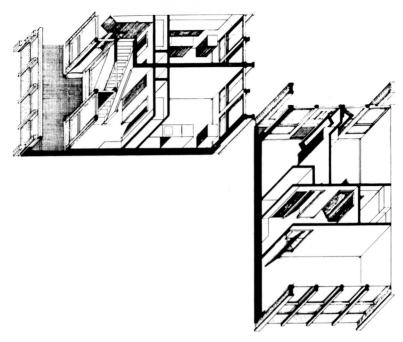

186. Robin Hood Lane. Axonometric drawing of three-person dwelling. Kitchen at same level as access deck, living-room on noisy side allows for two zones of use as it is long and thin and lit from the long side. Façade mullions are part of the scheme's protection against noise

The important differences between the Robin Hood Lane scheme and our earlier housing projects are:

First, in one important detail (fig. 186) the kitchen in the larger dwellings is at deck level to save lugging food and so on up the stairs; to make possible the supervision of small children playing outside the front door; and somehow to 'normalise' the dwelling.

Second, we have given the highest priority to making as large as possible 'inviolable' quiet open space that all share.[52] For since the first deck studies in 1952 we have become in our bodies aware of the stresses that urban noise and traffic movement induce, and realise that for the present time our most important need is for quiet places. To achieve a calm pool in this particular place, we have played down that idea of 'linkage' which was the main theme of the earlier 'Golden Lane' studies. In a sense we have replaced an image of the city in which connectedness was stressed, with one in which the survival of the 'person' and the 'thing' within the

[52] It is the size of that at Gray's Inn, which as near as anything can be is the model for this whole operation

194

ever-changing communications net is held to be pre-eminent.

Third, and in support of the above, all on-site movement of vehicles takes place in a 'moat', thereby screening off their noise and presence.

Fourth, only a few of the largest dwellings have 'yard-gardens' up in the air with them. In the rest the bedrooms can be opened up to the stress-free central zone.

Fifth, the design of the skin of the building is developed as part of the series of protective devices against noise – dwelling to dwelling as well as external sources.

[Overleaf; two fold-outs of Robin Hood Gardens]

Layout of Robin Hood Gardens, and road elevations
to Cotton Street and Robin Hood Lane

Source-list of illustrations

Many of these have had to be reproduced from faded tear-sheets and clippings, accumulated over twenty years. Hence the indifferent quality in several instances. If we have used copyright material without permission we apologise: it has proved impossible to identify and contact every source, despite our efforts.

A. & P.S.

Major G. W. G. Allen; Ashmolean Museum, Oxford, 58
Aerofilms, 2, 34, 60, 91, 114
Architects' Year Book 131, 143, 144
Architects Journal, 6
Ashmolean Museum, 58
Werner Bischof, 29
G. Douglas Bolton, 108
British Museum, 4
Emil Brunner, 25
Casabella, 95
The City of Tomorrow (Urbanisme), le Corbusier, 89
Crown copyright, 75
P. H. Davis, 100
The Earth, the Temple and the Gods, Scully, 79
Edinburgh Central Public Library, 11
Roger Fenton, Gernsheim Collection, 105
Fox Photos, 3
German Tourist Information Bureau, 134
Nigel Henderson, 21, 38, 69, 80
Dr St Joseph, Crown copyright, 59
Keystone, 50, 51, 81

Ladies Home Journal, 173
Life, 10, 112
Mainichi Daily News, 141
Felix H. Man, 63
Mississippi Stern Wheelers, Way Jr., 5
National Gallery, London, 62
Hans Namuth, 68
Oeuvre complète 1929–34, le Corbusier, 7, 90
Oeuvre complète 1938–46, le Corbusier, 76
Oeuvre complète 1952–57, le Corbusier, 156
Our World from the Air, Gutkind, 28
Perspecta 2, 130
Punch, 15
Radio Times Hulton Picture Library, 73
Saturday Evening Post, 104
A. and P. Smithson, 16, 18, 19, 20, 23, 24, 52, 93, 126, 127, 128, 129, 166
Studio Year Book 1919, 106
This is Tomorrow catalogue, 109
Time, 53
L'Unité d'habitation de Marseille, le Point, 74
U.S.I.S. London, 137
Anthony Wood, 14

Index